Mrs. Wilkes'
Boardinghouse
Cookbook

Mrs. Wilkes'
Boardinghouse
Cookbook

Recipes and Recollections from Her Savannah Table

With a History by
John T. Edge

Ten Speed Press
Berkeley   Toronto

VWM

Ten Speed Press
Box 7123
Berkeley, California 94707
www.tenspeed.com

Distributed in Australia by Simon & Schuster Australia,
in Canada by Ten Speed Press Canada, in New Zealand by
Southern Publishers Group, in South Africa by Real
Books, in Southeast Asia by Berkeley Books, and in the
United Kingdom and Europe by Airlift Book Company.

This is a **Design Press** book
Design Press is a division of the
Savannah College of Art and Design

Library of Congress Cataloging-in-Publication Data

Wilkes, Sema.
    Mrs. Wilkes' Boardinghouse cookbook : recipes
and recollections from her Savannah tables / with a
history by John T. Edge.
      p. cm.
Includes index.
ISBN 1-58008-257-2
I. Cookery, American—Southern style. I. Edge,
John T.   II. Mrs. Wilkes' Boardinghouse
(Restaurant)   III. Title.

TX715.2.S68 W48 2001
641.5975—dc21

Printed in Hong Kong
First printing, 2001

2 3 4 5 6 7 8 9 10 — 06 05 04 03 02 01

Cover and book design by Janice Shay and Winslett Long

Copyediting by Cameron Spencer and Elizabeth
Hudson-Goff

Research, development, and recipe testing by Marcia
Thompson and Carole Scott

John Mariani quote on p. 32: from *The Dictionary of American
Food and Drink* (William Morrow, 1994)

Craig Claiborne quote on p. 43: from *Craig Claiborne's
A Feast Made for Laughter* (Henry Holt & Company, 1983)

Anne Tyler quote on p. 59: from *Celestial Navigation*
(Alfred Knopf, 1974)

        Photography legend: t = top, b = bottom

Principal food photography by Deborah Whitlaw:
p. 8; p. 17; p. 31; p. 57; p. 67; p. 77; p. 81; p. 87;
p. 99; p. 105; p. 107; p. 111; p. 113; p. 117; p, 121;
p. 123; p. 129; p. 137 (t); p. 141; p. 149; p. 155;
p. 159

Additional photography by Zola Delburn:
p. 2; p. 33; p. 41; p. 45; p. 47; p. 68; p. 70; p. 71;
p. 78; p. 90; p. 94; p. 100; p. 137 (b); p. 168

Archival photographs by the Georgia Historical
Society, Cordray - Foltz Collection:
p. 12; p. 13 (t); p. 22; p. 25; p. 37; p. 38; p. 85;
p. 104; p. 119

Photograph by Savannah College of Art and Design;
Star Kotowski: p. 13

© *Esquire,* November 1970: p. 53

© *Atlanta Journal-Constitution* photo by Billy Downs,
September 15, 1975: p. 55 (b)

Photograph by Cam Dorsey Adams: p. 72

Photograph by Kristin Despatric: p. 82

V & J Duncan Antique Maps and Prints, Savannah,
Georgia: p. 97

Photograph by Bruce Feiler: p. 145

Photograph by Savannah College of Art and Design;
Chia Chong: p. 175

Contents

We dedicate this book to all the friends and customers whom it has been our pleasure to know and serve throughout these past sixty years and, especially, to our Mr. L. H. Wilkes, "Papa," who is greatly loved and missed.

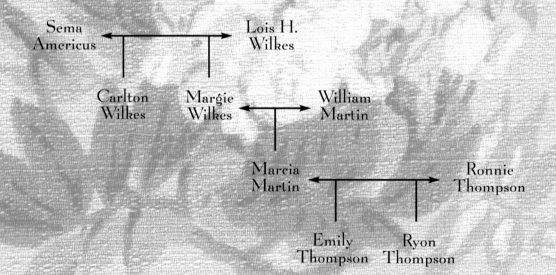

Sema
Americus

Lois H.
Wilkes

Carlton
Wilkes

Margie
Wilkes

William
Martin

Marcia
Martin

Ronnie
Thompson

Emily
Thompson

Ryon
Thompson

An Appreciation

There was a time not too long past when, if asked where to dine in the South, the first words to come spilling from my mouth were not "Mrs. Wilkes' Boardinghouse in Savannah, Georgia." Over the course of the past year, I have spent many happy hours at Mrs. Wilkes' table and, as a result, have come to appreciate the error of my ways.

How jaded was my palate, how blind was I to history, that I had not recognized Mrs. Wilkes' for what it is: perhaps the South's most venerable family restaurant, a modern-day reliquary of old-fashioned country cookery, where the tables groan beneath the weight of a midday repast and history stands still on the plate for all to admire.

Just this day, I sat down to a feast of fried chicken sheathed in a soft, blonde crust flecked with black pepper, butterbeans swimming in pot-likker, sweet creamed corn, ropy stewed okra, dusky collard greens, soft whorls of mashed sweet potatoes brightened with raisins, and bone-white biscuits that cleave in two with the slightest prod. In total, thirteen bowls of vegetables and three platters of meats blanketed the oilcloth-clad table, not to mention two baskets of coarse cornbread. As for the other seven tables, they too were crowded with food, and surrounded by intent eaters. To slake my thirst, I drank sweet tea from tall, sweaty glasses. For dessert, they passed monkey bowls full of sunshine-yellow banana pudding, studded with vanilla wafers, and I ate my fill.

It is a typical summer afternoon on West Jones Street, a wide brick boulevard lined with regal, redbrick townhouses and somber, nineteenth-century brownstones framed by filigrees of wrought

iron. Moss hangs from the gnarled boughs of the live oak trees that span the street, swirling in the breeze like silvery tinsel bleached a dull gray by the sun. A line of hungry customers snakes back from the front door of the dining room along the ancient brick sidewalk. Though neon-hued nasturtiums bloom in the window boxes, and honeysuckle climbs the fence by the lane, their scents are lost in a savory fog that spirals upward from the kitchen chimney, smelling of country-cured ham and sweet stewed cabbage.

Inside, four generations of the Wilkes family work the ground-floor, brick and wainscot-walled dining room at 107 West Jones. Home from college for the summer, Emily and Ryon Thompson, the great-grandchildren of family matriarch Sema Wilkes, pour tea and greet customers. Their father, Ronnie, works the phones, ordering

At age ninety-four she is the queen of all she surveys, the grande doyenne of Southern dining.

corn by the bushel and okra by the crate, all the while keeping up a steady banter with the kitchen staff. Ronnie's wife, Marcia, grand-daughter of Mrs. Wilkes, stops in to lend a hand during the lunch rush. Her father, Bill Martin, works the cash register, while her mother, Margie, perches on a ladder-back chair, poring over the accounting ledgers.

That's Mrs. Wilkes over by the oak bureau, a cupcake of a woman, her face framed by a poof of gray curls. At age ninety-four she is the queen of all she surveys, the grande doyenne of Southern dining. And her adoring customers know it. Like supplicants to the altar, they approach, pen in hand, hoping to secure an autograph or glean a recipe. Some came to know Mrs. Wilkes and her restaurant only recently when she was awarded the James Beard America's Regional Classics Award. Others are regulars who were weaned on her stewed okra, reared on her meatloaf and mashed potatoes.

She smiles at all, winks at some, gives a pinch on the elbow to a precious few, and avoids questions with grace and good humor. Ask her how her little dining room came to be known internationally, how she came to fry chicken in Belgium and bake biscuits in Japan, how she came to be celebrated as the "Julia Child of country cooking," and she'll fix you with a slight, engaging smile and say, without a trace of irony, "One came and told another; it happened like that." Ask her the secret to the biscuits that Craig Claiborne once praised as "one of the greatest things, ever, to happen in my life," and she'll say, "The recipe is in my cookbook. How many would you like?" Tell her that her dining room has inspired a new generation of restaurant chefs and served as a sort of living history museum of Southern cookery for legions of vacationing outlanders, and she'll ask, "Would you like some more chicken, maybe another biscuit?"

At a time when only 55% of all restaurants last even three years, Sema Wilkes will soon celebrate her sixth decade of serving country cooking, rich with history, steeped in tradition, unsullied by pretense. Ever since the day in 1943 when she took over the reins of a nondescript railroad boardinghouse on a sun-dappled brick street off Pulaski Square in downtown Savannah, Mrs. Wilkes has worked hard to secure a reputation for fine food and good service, one simple, honest meal at a time. That she continues to thrive today at the age of 94 is a tribute to the love and support of a strong family and a dedicated staff with whom I had the great pleasure of working.

Mrs. Wilkes, thank you for inviting me to your table. I can't remember when last I have eaten so well or learned so much. I hope that the following text does you proud—and in so doing illuminates an important chapter in American culinary history.

John T. Edge
August 1, 2000

Boardinghouse Ruminations

A century ago, even fifty years ago, most Southern towns boasted a boardinghouse, maybe even two or three or more, where a drummer with a trunk full of gewgaws or a Bible salesman with a gold tooth and a sincere smile could expect to find a simple, quiet room furnished with a clean, iron bed, and a communal dining room that offered at least two hearty meals a day.

In those days, boardinghouses fed more than just itinerants. In contrast to the major cities where old-line restaurants served continental cuisine to the elite, boardinghouse food was *de rigueur* daily fare for locals, among them young, working-class laborers, spinster schoolteachers, widowed bankers, washerwomen, and middle-aged, middle-class merchants alike.

Of course, there were some homes where the food could be dismissed as the work of a slattern with a greasy skillet, but more often than not, the collard greens that showed up on the table Wednesday afternoon had been picked by the cook that morning and flavored with a bit of fatback from a hog her cousin killed and quartered a few months back. Come breakfast time, the eggs came from the henhouse around back, the syrup from a friend out in the country with a patch of sugarcane, the grits from a local miller who had a way with corn and a stone burr.

Such has ever been the case with the food at Mrs. Wilkes' Boardinghouse, a Savannah, Georgia, institution since the 1940s. At the time Sema Wilkes took over the reins, the previous proprietor, Mrs. Dennis Dixon, was already in her eighties and had been serving the public for a good thirty years. Mrs. Wilkes picked up right where she left off, cultivating

OPPOSITE: SEMA WITH HUSBAND, LOIS, AND DAUGHTER, MARGIE, IN 1926.

relationships with nearby farmers who dug sweet potatoes for her in the fall and shelled whippoorwill peas in the summer.

BOARDINGHOUSES RELIED ON FRESH PRODUCE, SUCH AS GREEN BEANS GROWN ON SOUTH GEORGIA FARMS.

The middle years of the twentieth century were the last great gasps of the boardinghouse glory days in Georgia, when visitors to the Blue Ridge Mountains in the northern region of the state considered a trip incomplete unless it included a stop at the Dillard House, when businessmen in Atlanta made the trip east from downtown to sup at Mrs. Hull's in Inman Park, when travelers to Macon couldn't resist the linen-shrouded baskets of biscuits served piping hot at the Butler House over on Poplar Street, when trainmen passing through the little burg of Climax in deepest southwest Georgia couldn't get enough of the meringue-crowned lemon pies at the Harrell House.

Today, such accommodations are scarce to nonexistent. The standardization of the lodging industry, spurred in large part by the success of Memphis, Tennessee's Holiday Inn Corporation, sounded the death knell for most of the old-style boardinghouses. The Dillard House upgraded to a mountain resort. Mrs. Hull's closed in the 1980s. Ditto the Butler House down in Macon and the Harrell House in Climax. A way of life, a focal point for community interaction, was on the wane.

And what of Mrs. Wilkes'?

Mrs. Wilkes' has continued to thrive as a boardinghouse-style restaurant, even after banishing the actual roomers. By the early 1970s, lines were forming out front before mealtime. Locals and in-the-know tourists began to whisper that hers was one of the last bastions of true boardinghouse fare, one of the few places left where one sat down next to perfect strangers to consume a pluperfect meal.

And then in 1976, Mrs. Wilkes and her daughter, Margie, released the first edition of a self-published cookbook, *Famous Recipes*. Initially available only at the restaurant, at the Bargain Corner grocery, and at a ladies' apparel shop known as Lady Jane, the cookbook sold out of first one printing

TRAINMEN WERE MRS. WILKES' FIRST REGULAR BOARDERS AND HUNGRY CUSTOMERS.

and then another. Today, more than 250,000 copies are in print. Needless to say, the recipes in that spiral-bound workhorse of a book form the core of this work of history, cookery, and culture.

Over the course of the ensuing two-plus decades, the lines at Mrs. Wilkes' have grown ever longer, and the good press just keeps rolling in, even as other storied boardinghouses close up shop for the final time. What made Mrs. Wilkes' different? To be sure, four generations of strong family stewardship had something to do with it. But it also seems that Mrs. Wilkes was fortunate in that she managed to hold on just long enough to tap into a nascent Southern nostalgia

WHERE IS MRS. WILKES' BOARDINGHOUSE? JUST LOOK FOR THE LINE OF PEOPLE ON WEST JONES STREET.

for the old ways, a nostalgia that perhaps reached full flower earliest in Savannah, where preservation efforts and ancestor worship took on all the trappings of a secular religion.

Though the Wilkeses were one of the first families to join arms with the Historic Savannah Foundation, they have never considered their business to be a relic of days past. "I enjoy feeding people," says Mrs. Wilkes. "This

is a business. It's as simple as that. The good Lord has been kind to us; I had a rough childhood and I wanted better for my children and grandchildren and their children too. I was determined that things would be different for them and this was all I had, all I could depend upon. I guess we did all right," she says with a wink and a slight, kind smile.

A Word about Savannah

When James Oglethorpe, trustee for the colony of Georgia, staked his claim on a February morning in 1733, he selected a spot on a forty-foot bluff overlooking the Savannah River some seventeen miles from the Atlantic coast. "The last and fullest consideration of the Healthfulness of the place was that an Indian nation, who knew the Nature of the Country, chose it for their Habitation," he later reported to the colony's sponsors in England.

With the possible exception of two figures—Sema Wilkes, of course, and author John Berendt, whose nonfiction portrait of the city, *Midnight in the Garden of Good and Evil,* rankled the elite and summoned a stampede of curious tourists—Oglethorpe has enjoyed the most profound effect of any one person on the city of Savannah. "The river has formed a half moon," he wrote in 1733, "around the side of which the banks are about forty feet high, and on the top a flat which they call a bluff. . . . Upon the river-side, in the center of the plain, I have laid out the town, opposite to which is an island of very rich pasturage. The river is pretty wide, the water fresh, and from the quay of the town you can see its whole course to the sea." Oglethorpe's city plan endures to this day, a regimental grid of streets and public squares

BOTH MRS. WILKES AND AUTHOR JOHN BERENDT STIMULATED INTEREST IN THIS GRAND OLD SOUTHERN CITY.

that gives a human scale to this city of 150,000-plus.

Oglethorpe's idyll was short-lived. By 1743 he returned to England, never to see Savannah or Georgia again. In the ensuing years, his vision of a utopian community free from slaveholding or land speculation would succumb to economic and political pressures as the slave-fueled crops of rice and indigo replaced ill-fated attempts to raise grapes and harvest silk.

By the time of the Revolutionary War, Savannah was a thriving seaport. Its location, at the tail end of the thirteen colonies, however, left it susceptible to attack, and in December of 1778, it was captured by the British, remaining in the hands of the redcoats until after the close of the war.

The years between the Revolutionary War and the Civil War would prove to be Savannah's heyday as the business of cotton brought untold wealth to the port city. It was also during this period that the city's residents began constructing many of the elegant homes that now grace the town squares. By 1820, Savannah could boast of being one of the twenty largest cities in the United States.

During the Civil War, Union blockades severed Savannah's trade routes, but the city did not suffer the physical damage that many Georgia towns did. Instead, the "Hostess City of the South" remained above the fray, enduring Northern occupation as if it were an extended visitation from a particularly uncouth cousin rather than the quartering of an invading army.

During World War II, Savannah's shipyards built boats by the score to contribute to American naval power. And during the Civil Rights Movement, black Savannahians, through a series of well-executed economic boycotts, won a series of decisive battles in the struggle for equal accommodation under the law.

But the real story of Savannah in the modern era is reflected not by what has changed but, rather, by what has endured. Foremost among the many jewels in Savannah's cultural crown is Sema Wilkes' tidy, ground-floor dining room on West Jones Street. There, every noon, you can count on finding silk-clad swells and coverall-clad construction workers alike tucking into a timeless, tasty Southern repast and washing it all down with iced tea so sweet that it'll make your molars ache.   —J. T. E.

THE TABLE IS SET. IT'S 11 A.M. AND TIME TO OPEN THE DOOR TO THE FIRST EAGER DINERS.
IN MOMENTS, MRS. WILKES WILL OFFER THE DAILY MEALTIME BLESSING,
AS SHE HAS DONE FOR THE PAST FIFTY-EIGHT YEARS.

*"Good Lord,
bless this food to us,
and us to thy service.
Amen."*

Appetizers
and
Soups

Life on the Farm at Aimwell

The twentieth century was but seven years old when little Sema Americus Morris was born to William Lawton Morris and Emily Taylor Morris on a warm June day. Her family were farmers. Lawton worked a patch of loamy soil in the Aimwell community, just outside the town of Vidalia in southeastern Georgia. Emily ran the household, cooking for field hands and family alike on a wood-burning stove.

Sema was their first child, though two sons, Floyd and Colon, would follow in quick succession. Life revolved around the seasonal cycles of agriculture. In the fall, W. L. Morris harvested tobacco; in winter he cured hams and smoked sausages, which he bartered for sugar and wheat flour. Come spring, he worked to break the crop rows with a mule-drawn plow. In the summer he tended a patch of squash and peppers, beans, and peas.

Sema made her debut at a time when the first pearly ears of white summer corn were coming in, when fat, red-ripe orbs hung heavy from the stalks of dusky-green tomato plants. Her first few years were idyllic, days on end spent gathering nuts beneath the boughs of the towering pecan trees that ringed the family farmhouse, fashioning corn shuck dolls by the light of a kerosene lantern, or rocking the evening away on the front porch with family and friends. Her aunt and uncle lived just across the branch, her paternal grandmother and grandfather just down the road. All was good, all was right. But when her mother took to her bed, heavy with her fourth child and fading fast, young Sema's perfect little world came crashing down around her.

THE FIRST CHILD BORN TO WILLIAM LAWTON MORRIS AND EMILY TAYLOR MORRIS, SEMA POSES WITH HER BROTHERS AND HER DOLL.

"Momma asked me to come over to her bedside," Sema Wilkes recalls,

THE MORRIS FAMILY HOMESTEAD.

nearly ninety years hence. "I was only seven. She told me what to do to get dinner on the table for my father and the other men when they came in from the fields. I learned to stand on my tiptoes at her stove to stir the pots, and I milked the cows so we had butter. I've still got a big ole thumb from doing all that milking. When my mother died, I cried and cried and cried. My mother was a kind, sweet person. She was fair complected and tall like my daughter, Margie. I loved her so much. But when my father remarried, his new wife had a mean disposition. I wasn't used to that. I remember taking all my clothes and just cutting them to pieces. I was mad; I wanted my mother."

By the time Sema reached the age of twelve, tragedy struck again: Her father died of cancer. In short time, her aunt and uncle stepped into the breach, raising Sema and her two brothers as if they were their own, though her time under their roof would be short. "I met Mr. Wilkes when I was in the sixth grade," she recalls. "He was a handsome man, tall and kind. When we married, I was sixteen and he was eighteen. We took off in a horse and buggy to see the justice of the peace and spent the night with a cousin and his wife out in the country."

For the next twenty-odd years, Sema and L. H. Wilkes worked their own patch of soil. Like their parents before them, they farmed, gathering pecans to pay their taxes, taking their corn to a nearby mill to be ground into sacks of meal and grits, digging sweet potatoes and picking collards to be bartered for the few things that they couldn't raise on the farm.

During the early years of their marriage, Sema Wilkes gave birth to

SEMA AND L. H. RAISED
THEIR OWN CORN AND
OTHER CROPS FOR
CONSUMPTION AND
TRADE. IN THE FALL,
THEY SLAUGHTERED ONE
OF THEIR HOGS FOR
FOOD AND SOAP.

two children: Margie in 1926 and Carlton in 1932. "We were brought up in the middle of the Depression," recalls Margie, "but I don't remember being poor. We ate biscuits at every meal, and it seems somebody was always making a fruitcake, stirring it up in a big old washpan and mixing in oranges and lemons and all sorts of things. And when we had relatives in town, we really ate. Mother would fix them a big breakfast on the morning they were going to leave. We'd have eggs and bacon or fatback and biscuits all the time, but on special occasions, she might fry up a chicken or a steak too. What we didn't eat went into the pie safe for the next meal. We never went without."

For the Wilkes clan, frugality was a way of life, not a temporary condition. Each year, not long after the first frost, Mr. Wilkes would gather together with family and friends to kill and quarter a hog. Margie remembers it as a time of celebration: "They would make all kinds of delicacies from that hog. My father would make souse meat and liver pudding, things you couldn't

buy but everyone just loved. And of course we salted our own bacon and hung up our hams. And my grandmother—my father's mother—would make soap from the lard. It's kind of hard to explain, but those were festive times; that was a big deal."

But festive times for the Wilkes family were again short-lived. Life on the farm came to an abrupt end in 1942. The United States had entered the ongoing world war, and military bases and airfields began springing up around the South. One day in the spring of 1942, the Wilkes family was served notice that their land had been condemned, claimed by the federal government. A new airfield was coming in.

"There wasn't much we could do," recalls Mrs. Wilkes. "Mr. Wilkes lit off for Savannah to try and find a job in the shipyards. And I came down on the weekends to visit. It wasn't too long before he settled in at Mrs. Dixon's boardinghouse. When I agreed to help her out for a bit, I never expected to be still here, in the same spot, nearly sixty years later."

—J. T. E.

CARLTON WILKES, SON OF SEMA AND L. H., STANDS IN FRONT OF THE FORSYTH PARK FOUNTAIN IN 1943, THE SAME YEAR SEMA BEGAN SERVING FOOD TO BOARDERS.

Appetizers

ARTICHOKE DIP

Served hot, this easy, quick dip—a popular standard at many Southern get-togethers—is perfect to sate any guest's anxious appetite.

1 cup mayonnaise
1 cup grated Parmesan cheese
1 (14-ounce) can artichoke hearts, drained and chopped
Pinch of garlic powder

Preheat the oven to 350°. Combine all of the ingredients in a small casserole. Bake, covered, for 15 to 20 minutes. Serve with wheat crackers. Yields about 3 cups.

CRAB DIP

Come summer, the Wilkes family heads to the beach. Leftover crabs pulled fresh from the traps at Tybee always turn up in this delectable dip.

1/2 pound crabmeat
1 (8-ounce) package cream cheese, softened
3 tablespoons mayonnaise
1 small onion, chopped
1/2 teaspoon Worcestershire sauce
1 tablespoon horseradish
Sliced almonds

Mix all of the ingredients in a microwave-safe bowl. Microwave until the cheese is melted. Serve with crackers. Yields about 2 cups.

ANGELS ON HORSEBACK

Known in some Southern circles as Confederates on Horseback.

1 pint select shucked oysters
12 strips bacon, sliced in half
1/2 teaspoon salt
1/8 teaspoon pepper
1/8 teaspoon paprika
2 tablespoons chopped parsley

Preheat the oven to 450°. Wash and drain the oysters and lay each oyster across strip of bacon. Sprinkle with the salt, pepper, paprika, and parsley. Roll the bacon around the oyster and fasten with a toothpick. Place in a shallow baking pan on the lower rack and bake for about 10 minutes, or until the bacon is crispy. Remove the toothpicks and serve. Serves about 6.

MRS. WILKES BOUGHT FRESH PRODUCE AND MEAT AT THE OLD CITY MARKET IN DOWNTOWN SAVANNAH.

SHRIMP DIP

The Wilkes family prefers local Georgia medium whites because larger ones tend to be tougher. The warm water of Georgia makes Georgia shrimp especially tasty and tender.

1 (3-ounce) package cream cheese, softened
2 tablespoons mayonnaise
1 tablespoon catsup
1 tablespoon prepared mustard
Pinch of garlic powder
1 cup minced cooked shrimp
1/4 cup minced celery
1 teaspoon minced onion

Combine the cream cheese, mayonnaise, catsup, mustard, and garlic powder and blend until smooth. Stir in the shrimp, celery, and onion. Mix well. Serve with your favorite crackers. Serves 8.

HOMEMADE CRISPY CRACKERS

A recipe inspired by the crackers once served at the DeSoto, grand old hotel and former locus of Savannah's social life.

2 1/4 cups self-rising flour
1/4 cup sugar
1/2 teaspoon salt
1/2 cup butter or margarine, softened
8 ounces plain yogurt

Preheat the oven to 350°. Combine the flour, sugar, and salt. Stir in the butter. Add the yogurt and mix in a food processor. This will make a soft dough. Break off pieces and roll out on a floured board until you have a very thin sheet. Place on an ungreased cookie sheet and bake for 5 minutes. Turn off the oven and sprinkle salt on the crackers. Leave in the oven until cool; they will be very crispy. When cool, carefully lift the sheets and break into serving-sized pieces. Serves 12.

CHEESE BALLS

From the recipe files of Margie Martin, daughter of Mrs. Wilkes.

1 pound mild or sharp Cheddar cheese, grated
1 (8-ounce) package cream cheese, softened
1 cup chopped nuts
1/2 teaspoon garlic powder
Chile powder (optional)

Combine the Cheddar and cream cheeses in a mixing bowl and mix until well blended. Add the nuts and garlic and mix. Shape into bite-sized balls. If you like spicy foods, roll lightly in chile powder. Yields 3 dozen.

CRACKER NIBBLES

This is a quick party pass-around recipe on Savannah's cocktail circuit.

1/2 cup corn oil
1/2 package dried buttermilk salad dressing mix
1/2 teaspoon garlic salt
1/2 teaspoon lemon pepper
1/2 teaspoon dill weed
1 large box oyster crackers

Combine the oil, dressing mix, garlic salt, pepper, and dill weed in a small saucepan. Cook over low heat; do not boil. Pour over the crackers in a plastic bowl with a top. Shake and turn the bowl to coat the crackers well. Delicious served with other party snacks. Serves 6 to 8.

"If you've got good food at a fair price, you don't need all that other stuff. It's pretty hard to eat atmosphere."

—MRS. WILKES

Appetizer Tomato Sandwiches

You can't grow up in the South without vine-ripened tomato sandwiches! Pick the plumpest, reddest tomatoes you can find—grocery-store balsa-wood-textured varieties are not acceptable under any circumstances!

2 loaves (about 24 slices) sandwich-style white bread
4 medium vine-ripened tomatoes
1 medium Vidalia onion, finely chopped
1 cup mayonnaise
1/4 teaspoon salt
1 teaspoon ground pepper
Finely chopped fresh basil or parsley

Cut each slice of bread with a 2 1/2-inch biscuit cutter, then cut half of the slices again with a 1-inch cutter to create a hole for the garnish. Cut each tomato into 6 slices; drain on paper towels while preparing the filling. Combine the onion, mayonnaise, salt, and pepper in a small bowl. Lightly spread over both sides of each sandwich round. To assemble a sandwich, top 1 slice of bread with a tomato slice and then top with a cut-out slice of bread. Sprinkle basil or parsley on top. Yields 24 sandwiches.

Soups

Chilled Fruit Soup

8 cups orange juice
8 tablespoons quick-cooking tapioca
1/4 cup sugar
Pinch of salt
1/4 cup lemon juice
5 cups diced fresh or frozen fruit (peaches, bananas, melon, blueberries, or raspberries)

Mix the orange juice and tapioca in a large saucepan and let set for 10 minutes. Bring to a boil, stirring constantly. Remove from the heat and add the sugar, salt, and lemon juice. Cool, stirring once after 20 minutes. Cover and chill. Add the fruit and serve. Serves 6 to 8.

Oyster Stew

The Wilkes family could always rely on Frank Mathews, the local fishmonger, for quarts of fresh-shucked select oysters. Savannahians dote on these in the "R" months—what could be better on a chilly winter evening?

1/2 pint washed and shucked oysters
3/4 teaspoon salt
1/8 teaspoon pepper
1/4 cup butter or margarine
1 quart milk

Pick the oysters for bits of shell. Reserve the oyster liquor. Place in a colander and run cold water through the oysters. Add the salt, pepper, and butter and heat in a skillet until the edges of the oysters curl. Pour into milk that has been heated but not boiled. Add the oyster liquor. Simmer to a near boil. Add more pepper and pour into soup bowls. More salt, pepper, and butter may be added to taste. Serves 4.

Cream of Broccoli Soup

1/4 cup chopped onion
1/4 teaspoon tarragon
1 bunch fresh or 2 (10-ounce) packages frozen broccoli, chopped
2 quarts chicken stock
1/4 cup cornstarch
1 cup light cream
1/4 teaspoon curry powder
1/2 pound American cheese, grated
Salt and pepper

Add the onion, tarragon, and broccoli to the chicken stock. Simmer for 30 minutes. Mix the cornstarch, cream, and curry powder in a bowl. Add to the stock. Stir until creamy. Add the cheese, and season with salt and pepper to taste. Serves 8.

Brunswick Stew

Millie Parish, long-time cook at Mrs. Wilkes', claims this traditional huntsman's stew as her specialty.

2 pounds pork or chicken, chopped and cooked
1/2 teaspoon black pepper
1 teaspoon hot sauce
2 tablespoons Worcestershire sauce
1/3 cup pork or bacon drippings
1/2 cup vinegar-based barbecue sauce
1 1/2 cups catsup
2 cups diced potato, cooked
3 (12-ounce) cans cream-style corn

Place all of the ingredients in a saucepan, cover, and heat slowly. Salt and more hot sauce may be desired according to taste. Yields about 2 quarts.

Crab Stew

Local blue crabs are preferred, but recently stonecrabs are prevalent. "On our dock at Tybee," says granddaughter Marcia, "we pull stonecrabs up on the end of strings baited with chicken necks."

2 tablespoons butter or margarine
4 tablespoons flour
1 teaspoon salt
1/4 teaspoon white pepper
1 quart milk
1 tablespoon lemon juice
1/8 teaspoon Tabasco sauce
1 tablespoon Worcestershire sauce
1/2 cup crabmeat
1/4 cup sherry

Melt the butter in a medium saucepan; stir in the flour, salt, and pepper. Cook for 1 minute. Add the milk and heat until bubbly. Stir in the lemon juice, Tabasco, and Worcestershire. Cook until thickened. Add crabmeat and sherry just before serving. Serves 4.

AS APPEALING TO THE EYE AS TO THE PALATE, TOMATO ASPIC IS A PERFECT ACCOMPANIMENT TO BOTH HOT AND COLD MEALS. SEE RECIPE, PAGE 59.

According to John Mariani's *Dictionary of American Food and Drink*, this is a "nineteenth-century colloquialism referring to the need to reach quickly and decisively across a boardinghouse common dinner table or risk not getting any food. At such establishments the social graces were usually not observed, and grabbing at food was more the norm." One wonders if Mr. Mariani has ever had the pleasure of dining at Mrs. Wilkes' table, where decorum and deference rule.

—J. T. E.

SALMON SOUP

I small (7 1/2-ounce) can pink or red salmon, drained
1/4 cup butter or margarine
3 cups milk
Salt and pepper
Dash of Tabasco sauce (optional)

Place the salmon in a heavy saucepan. Add the butter and bring to a boil. Pour in the milk and stir while simmering to a near boil. Add the salt, pepper, and Tabasco. Serves 4.

SHRIMP BISQUE

One of the pragmatic cook's staples, cream of tomato soup is essential to create this easy, elegant bisque. The combination of shrimp and tomatoes is a signature of Savannah.

4 tablespoons butter or margarine
I small onion, finely chopped
2 teaspoons paprika
I teaspoon salt
1/2 teaspoon pepper
1/4 cup flour
2 cups light cream
I cup milk
I pound cooked shrimp
I (10 1/2-ounce) can condensed cream of tomato soup
1/2 cup white wine or sherry
I tablespoon lemon juice
Dash of Tabasco sauce

Melt the butter in a medium saucepan. Sauté the onion until soft; add the paprika, salt, and pepper. Cook for 1 minute. Add the flour and stir until smooth. Pour in the cream and milk and cook until thickened. Remove from the heat. Pour into a food processor; add the shrimp and blend until smooth. Return to the saucepan. Add the tomato soup, wine, lemon juice, and Tabasco. Heat until almost boiling. Serves 4 to 6.

TIME: HIGH NOON ON ANY GIVEN WEEKDAY. IN LESS THAN THREE HOURS THESE POTS AND PANS WILL BE EMPTY AGAIN.

ONION SOUP

A native of Toombs County—home of the super-sweet Vidalia onion—Mrs. Wilkes was frequently asked to judge onions. Vidalias always won.

1 pound Vidalia onions, minced
Butter
1 tablespoon flour
1 1/2 quarts chicken stock or beef broth
Bread crumbs
Grated Parmesan cheese

Sauté the onions in butter until brown. Stir in the flour and stock or broth. Let stand for several hours to improve the flavor. Place in individual ovenproof soup bowls and liberally sprinkle bread crumbs and Parmesan cheese on top. Place in the oven and bake until the soup is hot and the crumbs are toasted. Serves 6.

CAULIFLOWER SOUP

2 medium heads of cauliflower, broken into florets
1/2 cup butter or margarine
1 cup finely chopped celery
2 tablespoons grated onion
2 tablespoons flour
1 quart chicken stock
4 cups hot milk
Salt and pepper
2 egg yolks, beaten (optional)
3/4 cup grated mild or sharp Cheddar cheese (optional)

Boil the cauliflower until tender and mash or process in a blender. Melt the butter in a pot and cook the celery and onion for about 2 minutes. Stir in the flour but do not brown. Gradually add the chicken stock. Add the cauliflower and stir in the hot milk. Season with salt and pepper to taste. Stir over medium heat until the mixture coats the spoon. Remove from the heat and stir in the egg yolks. Sprinkle the cheese on top. Serves 8 to 10.

Sauces,
Dressings,
and
Relishes

Early Savannah Days

It wasn't supposed to work out this way," says Mrs. Wilkes. "Our family was living up in Toombs County, out from Vidalia, when the government wanted our farm for an air base. That was back in the summer of 1942. So my husband moved to Savannah to take a job in the shipyards, and when I came down on the weekends, well, we stayed at this boardinghouse. It was a railroad boardinghouse. Old Mrs. Dennis Dixon owned it then and was short on help. She asked would I help? I said I'd try, and one thing led to another and before too long, I bought her out. That was early in the winter of 1943. By the time we got settled in good, Mr. Wilkes was working as a trainman for the Seaboard Airline Railroad."

During the war years, Savannah was a boomtown, flush with troops bivouacked at nearby Fort Jackson and farmers from throughout southern Georgia who, like Mr. Wilkes, came to town in search of work in the shipyards or other war-related industries. At the time of the Wilkes family arrival, the Pulaski Square neighborhood where she kept house was rife with boardinghouses, says Mrs. Wilkes. "You know what they say about liquor stores? 'There's one on every corner.' Well, that's the way it was with the boardinghouses back then. Of course, I always thought we were the best of the bunch."

In those days, Savannah supported fifty or more boardinghouses, five alone on the 100 block of West Jones Street. Some were rambling clapboard or regal brownstone homes, lorded over by a proud Savannah lady of the old school. Maybe her husband had passed away, and rather than sell the family homeplace, she began taking in boarders. Maybe she had begun to take in roomers as a kindness at a time when public accommodations were few.

Other boardinghouses were dilapidated hovels, close to collapse, infamous flophouses populated by the down-and-out and the destitute, where men slept four and five to a room and the midday meal was, as one traveler of the same period put it, "nothing but hash and grease, grease and hash."

WEST JONES STREET ABOUT
THE TIME MRS. WILKES
ARRIVED IN SAVANNAH.

BECAUSE MOST BOARDINGHOUSES HAD NO PHONES, RAILROAD CALLBOYS PEDALED THEIR BIKES TO MRS. WILKES' TO ALERT THE RAILROAD MEN THAT THEIR TRAINS WERE READY TO DEPART.

"Mrs. Wilkes' Boardinghouse was different," recalls Sleepy Warren, a onetime railroad callboy, whose job it was to make the rounds on bicycle, rousing the brakemen and engineers and other railroad folk for their next run. "She had a reputation as having the best food from way back. All the railroad men loved her. They might have come because they knew Mr. Wilkes, but they stayed because of Mrs. Wilkes' good cooking."

"I believe they called Father a trainman," says Mrs. Wilkes' only daughter, Margie Martin. "He loved his work and never wanted to be a conductor or engineer. He got to where he enjoyed his seniority. He enjoyed getting off work when he needed to so that he could help mother out. But, oh, did he just love to talk with the other railroad men. They would sit outside on a swing and talk all day long."

Robbie Thompson, Ronnie's brother, recalls, "They always referred to Mr. Wilkes as Corn Bread. I guess he ate a lot of the stuff. He always seemed to be in good spirits, laughing and joking. And he was always popular with the other railroad men because he would load them up with groceries. Everybody loved to work with him. He always seemed to have a big brown paper sack with him, just filled with fried chicken and corn bread. He was devoted to the railroad and to that dining room. It was a combination of his good humor and Mrs. Wilkes' good cooking that made that little boardinghouse into what it is."

In the early days, the ground-floor dining room boasted just one table and twelve seats: one chair for each boarder and one for Mr. Wilkes. "I don't rightly recall when all that began to change," says Mrs. Wilkes. "As best as I can remember, we'd have one man that wanted to bring a friend and then another. Then neighborhood people started asking if they could eat with us too. That was when we served three meals every day but Sunday. I was happy to have the business because I always had a mind that I wanted to just serve meals. Those roomers were a lot of trouble, and there was no money in it."

One of the locals who came strolling by in search of a hot home-cooked midday meal was Bill Martin. "He worked at the Union Camp plant," recalls Margie. "He'd eat with us fairly often and before long I came to know that he was sweet on me. We married in 1945." In 1947, Margie and Bill Martin gave birth to a daughter, Marcia. "She was the apple of her grandfather's eye," says Margie. "He couldn't get enough of that child."

MR. AND MRS. WILKES AND MARCIA, 1948.

In succeeding years, a cast of neighborhood characters would come to call the dining room home, if only between the hours of 11:00 and 2:00, when Mrs. Wilkes and an increasing cadre of cooks set out a midday feast of baked ham, fried chicken, a bounty of Southern vegetables, and, on Fridays, fresh, local fried flounder. "We were known for our flounder," recalls Mrs. Wilkes. "Friday was the big day when everybody wanted in."

Meanwhile, changes were afoot in Savannah. The Pulaski Square neighborhood that the Wilkes family called home was on the wane. The old railroad men were dying off. As a new generation of Americans took to the roadways in gleaming Chevys and Fords, the railroad industry itself turned moribund. One by one, the other boardinghouses began to close their doors.

MRS. WILKES IN HER KITCHEN, 1950.

Though she did enjoy the company of her husband's railroad colleagues, Mrs. Wilkes saw her chance. "We made the decision to close the place to roomers back around about the time we bought the building," says Mrs Wilkes. "It was time for a change. Our business around noon was building so much that we added another couple of tables. Besides, I never liked all those men hanging around outside and talking away. It wasn't a good sight. One of the first things I did was take that bench they'd sit on and move it inside."   —J. T. E.

Sauces & Dressings

BROWN GRAVY

"We like our gravy cooked right in the skillet or roasting pan with the tiny browned bits scraped from the bottom of the pan," says Marcia Thompson. "This is the first thing you'll see when you sit down at the table, alongside a bowl of steaming white rice," adds Mrs. Wilkes.

2 tablespoons fat drained from meat stock
2 tablespoons flour
1 cups water
Kitchen Bouquet (optional)

Heat the fat to a boil in a pan, stir in the flour, and whisk until well blended. Quickly pour in the water and stir until well blended. Add more water if needed for the consistency you prefer. Add a touch of Kitchen Bouquet for extra color and flavor. Yields about 1 cup.
NOTE: Another tried and true gravy method is to shake the flour and water in a jar with a tight-fitting lid before adding to the hot fat. No lumps!

GIBLET GRAVY

This is sumptious over dressing, too.

3 tablespoons fat drained from meat stock
3 tablespoons flour
3 cups chicken or turkey stock
Chopped giblets, removed from stock
2 eggs, boiled and chopped
1/3 cup evaporated milk

Return the fat to the pan and simmer over low heat. Blend in the flour, stirring with a spoon until brown. Pour in the stock, giblets, and eggs. Stir until boiling. Add the evaporated milk and simmer until thick and smooth. Serves 12.

Milk Gravy

Mrs. Wilkes always serves this with biscuits and fried chicken, a splendid dish that dates back to her days on the farm.

3 tablespoons drippings drained from fried chicken
   or pork chops
3 tablespoons flour
1 cup milk
Salt and pepper

Heat the drippings. Add the flour, stirring while the mixture browns. Slowly add the milk as it thickens. Add hot water if the mixture becomes too thick. Season with salt and pepper to taste. Serve on rice or mashed potatoes. Yields 3 cups.

Swiss Cheese Sauce

1/2 cup grated Swiss cheese
1/4 cup mayonnaise or salad dressing
1/2 cup dairy sour cream
Pinch of paprika

Combine the cheese and mayonnaise. Simmer over low heat, stirring constantly, until the cheese melts. Stir in the sour cream and continue to heat. Add the paprika. Serve over hot cauliflower or asparagus. Yields 1 cup.

Mushroom Sauce

1/2 pound chopped mushrooms
2 tablespoons butter or margarine
1/4 cup flour
3 teaspoons salt
Pinch of pepper
2 cups milk or chicken broth
Snipped parsley

Sauté the mushrooms in the butter for 3 to 4 minutes. Stir in the flour, salt, and pepper. Add the milk. Continue to heat, stirring until thickened. Add the parsley. Yields about 2 cups.

Cocktail Sauce

1 teaspoon chile powder
1/4 teaspoon Tabasco sauce
1 tablespoon Worcestershire sauce
2 tablespoons lemon juice
1/2 teaspoon salt
1 cup catsup
1 1/2 cups chile sauce

Combine all of the ingredients and stir until well blended. Serve with your favorite seafood. Yields about 2 1/2 cups.

Cream Sauce

4 tablespoons butter or margarine
4 tablespoons flour
2 cups light cream or fresh whole milk
Salt and pepper
1/4 cup sherry

Melt the butter in a saucepan over low heat. Add the flour and cream. Stir until smooth, season with salt and pepper to taste, and add the sherry. Yields about 1 1/2 cups.
NOTE: Do *not* use sherry in creamed vegetables.

CRANBERRY SAUCE

For some Southerners, this is a Thanksgiving treat, but at Mrs. Wilkes', it has been a constant on the table since way back.

2 cups granulated sugar
2 cups water
1 pound (4 cups) fresh cranberries

Combine the sugar and water in a saucepan. Boil for 3 to 5 minutes. Add the cranberries. Bring to a boil, uncovered. Cook, without stirring, for about 5 minutes, until the cranberry skins pop open. Cool and keep refrigerated until ready to serve. Yields 1 quart.
NOTE: To enhance the flavor, try adding a pinch of cinnamon and 1/2 teaspoon vanilla.

SPICY BARBECUE SAUCE

At Mrs. Wilkes', Wednesday means Barbecue Pork, Thursday means Barbecue Chicken, and Friday means Barbecue Ribs, so you can bet that this sauce is important.

1 pint vinegar
Juice of 3 lemons
1/2 cup sugar
1 quart catsup
2 tablespoons salt
1/2 tablespoon cayenne pepper
3/4 tablespoon black pepper
3 tablespoons prepared mustard
Tabasco sauce (optional)

Combine the the vinegar, lemon juice, and sugar and bring to a boil. Add the remaining ingredients and boil for about 5 minutes. Yields about 6 cups.

Sweet and Sour Sauce

2 tablespoons soy sauce
1/2 cup brown sugar
1/4 cup vinegar
1/2 cup apricot nectar
1 tablespoon catsup
1/4 teaspoon dry mustard
1/4 teaspoon ground ginger
1/4 teaspoon salt
Tabasco sauce (optional)

Combine all of the ingredients in a saucepan and bring to a boil to the dissolve the sugar. Serve hot or cold on shrimp, pork, or anything your taste desires. Yields about 1 cup.

Blue Cheese Dressing

1/2 cup mayonnaise
1 cup dairy sour cream
1 clove garlic, crushed
6 tablespoons Italian dressing
1 teaspoon Worcestershire sauce
Salt
1 small (14-ounce) package blue cheese, crumbled

Setting 1/4 cup of the blue cheese aside, combine all of the ingredients, including salt to taste, and mix well. Cover, and refrigerate for at least 6 hours. Spoon onto salad and sprinkle the remaining 1/4 cup blue cheese on top. Yields about 1 3/4 cups.

Boardinghouse Salad Dressing

1 cup mayonnaise
1 cup sweet pickle relish, drained
2 cups French dressing

Stir the mayonnaise and relish into the French dressing until thoroughly mixed. Cover and refrigerate. Yields about 4 cups.

PICKLED BEETS, ONE OF MRS.
WILKES' PERSONAL FAVORITES AND
A DAILY FEATURE ON THE MENU.
RECIPE, PAGE 106.

From the Files

In 1973, David Brinkley
passed through Savannah and wanted
to film a feature story for the
NBC evening news. Mrs. Wilkes
agreed to let him do it if he
promised not to tell where her
dining room was located.

CRANBERRY ORANGE RELISH

1 pound (4 cups) fresh cranberries
2 oranges, quartered and seeded
2 cups granulated sugar

Chop the cranberries and oranges coarsely. Stir in the sugar and mix well. Refrigerate for several hours before serving. Yields 1 quart.

CURRIED FRUIT

"In the '40s and '50s when we couldn't get fresh fruit around the holidays, we served this as a companion to chicken and turkey. It became so popular, we keep on serving it today," says Margie. "You can, of course, substitute fresh fruit if you prefer, but you will have to adjust the cooking time."

1 large (20-ounce) can pineapple chunks
1 large (29-ounce) can peach halves
1 large (29-ounce) can pear halves
1 medium (15-ounce) can apricots
1 small (6-ounce) jar cherries
1/3 cup butter or margarine
3/4 cup light brown sugar
2 teaspoon curry powder

Drain the fruit. Place in a shallow baking dish. Melt the butter in a saucepan and add the brown sugar and curry powder. Spoon the mixture over the fruit. Cover and refrigerate for a few hours or overnight. Preheat the oven to 350°. Bake, uncovered, for 45 minutes. Serve warm with dinner. Serves 8 to 10.

CUCUMBER SLICES

4 to 6 cucumbers
1 cup white vinegar
1 teaspoon salt
1/2 teaspoon pepper
1 cup dairy sour cream (optional)

Peel the cucumbers and cut crosswise into very thin slices. Soak in ice water mixed with the vinegar, salt, and pepper. Remove the cucumbers after 30 minutes or more and pat dry on a towel. Serve with the sour cream. Serves 8 to 10. **NOTE:** For a more attractive dish, leave the cucumber unpeeled and score by running a fork down the side of the cucumber.

CRISP CUCUMBER PICKLES

50 small cucumbers, sliced
8 small onions, sliced or chopped
1/2 cup salt
5 cups sugar
5 cups white vinegar
1 teaspoon turmeric
1 tablespoon pickling spices

Mix the cucumbers, onions, and salt. Put in ice cubes and let stand for 3 hours. Combine the sugar and vinegar and bring to a boil. Drain the cucumbers and onions, and add them to the sugar and vinegar mixture. Add the turmeric and spices. When the mixture comes to a boil, pour into sterilized jars and seal. Chill. Yields about 6 to 8 quarts.

PEPPER VINEGAR

A cruet of this is always present on a Southern table, ever ready for sprinkling on greens.

1 quart fresh tiny green hot peppers
1 quart white vinegar

Pack the peppers into a 1-quart jar. Heat the vinegar to a boil. Pour the vinegar into the jar to cover the peppers. Seal the jar tightly and leave for several days. Use for seasoning greens and fish, or other vegetables and meats. The vinegar will keep for months. Yields about 4 1/2 pints.

BREAKFAST AS AN UNSUNG MEAL

Though the midday repast is the meal that has the multitudes lining the walk in front of Mrs Wilkes', breakfast is—forgive the pun—the sleeper meal: eggs, scrambled lightly and served from deep crockery bowls; grits, molten white gold, ladled on plates with a generous hand; hickory-smoked bacon, fried to a crisp; sausage links; sliced fruit; and, every once in a while, sliced tomatoes fresh from the garden. And don't you dare forget those ethereal blonde biscuits, just waiting to be slathered with butter or covered with cane syrup.   —J. T. E.

"I worked as a railroad callboy in Savannah from 1953 to 1956 or '57," says Sleepy Warren. "Back then the passenger station was over on what is now Martin Luther King, Jr. Boulevard, and the railroad hired callboys like me to get the men up and make sure they got to their trains. Most of the places didn't have phones, and we would pedal our bikes all across town to wake them men up when their train was ready to go. I had my own set of keys to the boardinghouses—had about 25 or 30 keys on a ring— and would just let myself in to get the brakemen, flagmen, conductors, all the men who bunked at the houses.

"There were five boarding-houses on Mrs. Wilkes' block alone. Catercorner from her was Brown's Café and Boarding-house. At 116 West Jones there was another. At 122 was Mrs. Tompkins'. Hundreds of men stayed in those old houses on Jones, Liberty, Huntington, Charlton, and Gaston streets. But none of them were ever quite like Mrs. Wilkes'. Hers always was the place to be."

WATERMELON PICKLES

Here's the answer to the eternal question: What do you do with the rind?

3 quarts watermelon rind from firm watermelons
Boiling water
7 cups granulated sugar
2 cups vinegar
2 teaspoons whole cloves
1 stick cinnamon, broken into pieces
1 small unpeeled orange
1 lemon

First day: Trim the green skin and any pink flesh off the watermelon rind. Cut the rind into 1-inch cubes. Place in a large saucepan and cover with boiling water. Boil for about 10 minutes, until tender; do not overcook. Drain well. Combine the sugar, vinegar, cloves, and cinnamon in another saucepan and bring to a boil. Pour over the rind. Let stand overnight at room temperature.

Second day: In the morning, drain the syrup from the rind into a saucepan. Heat to a boil and pour over the rind. Let stand overnight.

Third day: In the morning, slice the orange and lemon crosswise and quarter each slice. Add the orange and lemon to the watermelon rind mixture. Heat to a boil and immediately pour into 4 to 6 hot, sterilized pint jars. Seal and store in a cool, dry place. Yields 2 to 3 quarts.

PICKLED PEARS

This recipe works well with Georgia peaches, too.

5 pounds pears, quartered
1 1/2 pounds sugar
1 pint white vinegar
1 teaspoon ground ginger
2 sticks cinnamon
1 cup water
1 tablespoon whole cloves
2 slices lemon

Combine all of the ingredients in a large saucepan. Boil until the pears are tender when pricked with a toothpick. Pour into sterilized jars and seal. Yields about 4 pints.

GREEN TOMATO PICKLES

3 cups pickling lime powder
7 pounds green tomatoes, sliced
5 pounds sugar
3 pints pure apple vinegar
1 teaspoon each celery seed
1 teaspoon mace
1 teaspoon cinnamon
Green food coloring (optional)

Dissolve the lime powder in water. Cover and soak the tomatoes for 24 hours. Drain. Place the tomatoes in a pot and soak in fresh water for 4 hours, changing the water once every hour. Drain. Combine the sugar, vinegar, celery seed, mace, and cinnamon in a large saucepan and bring to a boil. Pour over the tomatoes. Let stand overnight. In the morning, boil for 1 hour and add green food coloring. Pour into sterilized jars and seal. Yields about 10 pints.

TOMATO RELISH

2 pounds tomatoes, chopped
1 medium green pepper, chopped
2 medium onions, minced
2 medium cucumbers, finely chopped
2 teaspoons salt
1 teaspoon dry mustard
1 teaspoon celery seed
1/4 cup vinegar
1/4 cup salad oil

Drain and combine the vegetables. Add the remaining ingredients and mix thoroughly. Refrigerate for several hours. Good with beef and fish. Yields 1 quart.

Strawberry Preserves

"We made these for our trip to New York in 1987 when Lord & Taylor paid homage to Savannah," remembers Marcia.

5 pounds firm ripe strawberries, washed and hulled
5 pounds sugar

Combine the strawberries and sugar in a pot. Slowly bring to a boil and boil for 8 minutes. Remove from the heat and let stand for 24 hours. Pour into sterilized jars and seal or place in a covered container and refrigerate. The strawberries will not shrink and will keep for at least 2 weeks refrigerated. Yields about 6 to 8 pints.

Pepper Jelly

Use as a condiment with cream cheese—a delicious spread on crackers!

2 cups puréed bell pepper
1/2 cup puréed hot pepper
1 1/2 cups white vinegar
7 1/2 cups sugar
1 bottle liquid pectin
Green food coloring (optional)

Bring the peppers, vinegar, and sugar to a boil. Cook for 6 minutes at a rolling boil. Remove from the heat and add the pectin. Boil for 3 more minutes. Add the food coloring and pour into sterilized jars and seal. Yields 3 pints.

 Salads

Boardinghouse Begets Restaurant

The middle years of the twentieth century were not kind to genteel old Savannah. Developers razed dozens of historic homes to make way for blacktop parking lots and garish corner convenience stores. Bricks that once graced fine Federal-style townhouses were trucked out to the suburbs for use in the building of the split-level ranch-style homes that were all the rage. Worst of all, three of the original twenty-four squares laid out in James Edward Oglethorpe's grand eighteenth-century plan for the city were paved slap over in an effort to aid the flow of traffic, to heed the call of so-called progress.

In response, an unlikely troupe of urban guerillas in pillbox hats and white gloves and seersucker suits worked to save what they could of Savannah's past grandeur, arranging for low-interest loans and tax abatements in exchange for purchaser agreements to restore and revitalize the once proud homes.

One of the first homes to be refurbished in concert with the Historic Savannah Foundation was the paired gray brick townhomes at 105–107 West Jones Street. Built in 1870 by Civil War veteran and cotton merchant Algernon S. Hartridge, the property was cited as a "stunning example of the style that can be accomplished with Savannah gray brick, double curving steps, and cast iron trim." To buy a home in the historic district was a bold move at the time, one that the family had not entertained before the establishment of the Historic Savannah Foundation, recalls Mrs. Wilkes. "We had never purchased the house because this area was fast becoming a slum." Indeed, it was a bold enough move that on November 24, 1965, when the Wilkeses signed the loan papers, the local news media were there to cover the event.

A little more than one year and many renovation missteps later, the house stood fully restored. Upstairs, the parlor floor was returned to its original scale: long, elegant rooms appointed with graceful, marble mantels. And on the two upper floors, a rabbit warren of smaller quarters was demolished to make way for roomy apartments. But downstairs, on the ground floor, where

Mrs. Wilkes performed her daily feats of culinary legerdemain, the look and feel of things remained much the same. "Just about all we did was move some posts around and remove some plaster so you could see the bricks on the wall down here," says Mrs. Wilkes. "I always have loved the look of brick."

Good food—country cooking come to town—remained the primary draw. Candied yams, snap beans, and zipper peas, fresh from a local garden; collard greens, butterbeans, and squash casserole bound with crushed corn flakes; white rice, brown rice, and red rice stoked with stewed tomatoes; fried chicken, baked ham, and country-fried steak pounded tender with a Coca-Cola bottle: despite the advancing years, the heady times, Mrs. Wilkes continued to serve up a timeless repast. And yet, ever so slowly, her clientele began to change, as grammar school teachers replaced railroad men, and itinerant drummers gave way to young bankers and younger college students.

In time, tourists also began to seek out the brick-walled downstairs dining room. Emboldened by articles published in *Esquire* and the *New York Times* and a profile broadcast by David Brinkley on the nightly news, they set out in search of what a small cadre of in-the-know chowhounds were touting as one of the best meals to be had in America. During those days, finding the restaurant was half the chore. Mrs. Wilkes took out no ads in

AN *ESQUIRE* MAGAZINE ARTICLE APPEARED IN NOVEMBER 1970, AND BROUGHT NATIONAL ATTENTION TO MRS. WILKES.

LONGTIME CUSTOMER,
I. J. JONES.

the newspaper. She posted no sign out front. Try to look up her address in the phone book and you found no notice in the yellow pages. Look in the white pages and if you were lucky, you might divine that a discreet listing— Wilkes, L. H. Mrs. 107 W Jones Street—was the clue you were searching for. Most eaters abandoned such culinary skullduggery and simply set out on foot for West Jones Street, trusting that if they followed their nose and asked enough questions, they would find their way to Mrs. Wilkes' door. Many cabdrivers made three and four daily runs of no more than two or three blocks, transporting famished diners who gave up their search.

As her fame grew, Mrs. Wilkes took it all in stride, remaining true to her roots. "The tourists come in here and are interesting," she told a reporter back in 1976. "But I don't want the tourists to ever crowd out the local people." To be sure, the locals kept coming, some with such regularity that they came to be considered extended members of the Wilkes clan. Mrs. Wilkes recalls regulars I. J. Jones and W. C. Dunn with a special fondness.

I. J. Jones was a retired railroad dispatcher who had worked alongside Mr. Wilkes. For the great majority of his adult life, Mrs. Wilkes' Boardinghouse was his de facto dining room, the place where he gathered with fellow retirees to swap stories and savor Mrs. Wilkes' good cooking. "I've been told I'm partly responsible for him being a bachelor," Mrs. Wilkes once remarked. "He just liked the food so well." Lytle Bevill, Jones's longtime girlfriend, agrees that Mrs. Wilkes might have had something to do with his status as an unrepentant bachelor. "He loved her food so," she recalls. "We met in Mrs. Wilkes' dining room along about 1946, when I was working on the corner at Harms Dairy. We both took our meals there and started to talk and then court. He was very proper, very distinguished. I never saw him without a suit or a sport coat and tie. He used to tell me, 'I don't feel dressed without a tie on.'"

Marcia Thompson remembers Mr. Jones as being a Wilkes' Boardinghouse fixture: "He was such a part of the place. He would help out, filling empty pitchers of tea or folding napkins. He was kind of courtly. And people loved to sit with him. They would ask after him when they came to eat. He was a sweetie." I. J. Jones passed away in March of 1997 at the age of eighty-five. "I was with him in the weeks just before he died," recalls Miss Bevill. "We would bring takeout from Mrs. Wilkes' to him every day, in his sickbed. He ate her food every day, until they had to put him in the hospital."

W. C. Dunn, on the other hand, was a veteran of the Spanish Civil War, given to wearing white gloves and a straw hat on summer days. Many longtime neighborhood residents recall seeing him, resplendent in a beige poplin suit, a walking cane fixed to his tricycle's crossbar, pedaling down the street, headed for a midday meal at Mrs. Wilkes'. Upon arrival by way of the rear lane, he would retrieve his cane from its resting place and stride proudly into the dining room at 11:30 on the nose, intent upon eating his fill of fried chicken and snap beans.

LOIS WILKES, KNOWN AS CORN BREAD TO HIS PALS, ENJOYED HELPING IN HIS WIFE'S DINING ROOM AND SWAPPING STORIES WITH OTHER RETIRED RAILROAD MEN.

By the early 1990s, he could claim to have eaten at Mrs. Wilkes' table each weekday for more than thirty years. Dunn finally parked his bike not long after celebrating his ninety-sixth birthday. He passed away shortly afterward. Countless other regulars of the old school could claim to be part and parcel of the fabric of that humble dining room when it was at its simplest and best.

It seemed to be time for the Wilkes clan to slow down a bit. But when Lois Wilkes retired his post as a railroad trainman, he declared that he was doing so, in part, to spend more time helping his wife with the chore of serving the hordes of locals and tourists now clamoring for her biscuits and gravy, her earthy black-eyed peas and oh-so-sweet banana pudding. For the next twenty-odd years, he was a constant presence in the dining room, always at hand to say grace when the first guests were seated, pull out a chair for a lady visitor, or share tales of exploits past with fellow railroad retirees who came by to sit a spell. "Mrs. Wilkes was devoted to him," recalls Marcia. "He was at the center of everything she did. Him and that dining room, that's all she seemed to think about." —J. T. E.

AT THE AGE OF NINETY-SIX, W. C. DUNN ARRIVES RIGHT ON TIME, READY FOR HIS DAILY FRIED CHICKEN AND SNAP BEANS.

Salads

DEVILED EGGS

6 hard-boiled eggs
I tablespoon mayonnaise
I tablespoon sweet pickle relish
I teaspoon pimientos, minced
I teaspoon French dressing
Salt and pepper

Cut the eggs in half and remove the yolks. Mash the yolks with a fork. Add the mayonnaise, relish, pimientos, and dressing to the yolks and mix. Season with salt and pepper to taste. Stuff eggs whites and refrigerate. Serves 6.

TUNA SALAD MOLD

This recipe calls for canned tuna, but 2 cups of fresh tuna can be substituted if you're lucky enough to have it on hand!

2 (7-ounce) cans tuna, drained
2 hard-boiled eggs, chopped
I/2 cup chopped ripe olives
I/2 cup sliced toasted almonds
I teaspoon unflavored gelatin
I/4 cup cold water
I cup mayonnaise or salad dressing
I cup dairy sour cream
I tablespoon grated onion
3/4 teaspoon salt
2 tablespoons lemon juice
I/2 cup chopped parsley
Lettuce
2 large tomatoes, quartered
I/3 cup chopped green pepper
I/2 cup chopped onion

Combine the tuna, eggs, olives, and almonds in a large mixing bowl. Soak the gelatin in the cold water for 5 minutes. Place in a double boiler over hot water until dissolved. Remove from the heat. Stir into the mayonnaise. Add the sour cream, the grated onion, salt, lemon juice, and parsley. Combine with the tuna mixture in a bowl and mix well. Pour into a ring mold and chill until firm. Unmold onto lettuce. Fill the center with tomatoes, green pepper, and chopped onion. Serves 6.

DEVILED EGGS

LITTLE EMILY THOMPSON WITH
HER GREAT GRANDMOTHER,
MRS. WILKES, AND FLORRIE
SIMPSON LEACH IN 1984.

Tango Salad

"Much as we prefer to use fresh ingredients, fresh pineapple will not allow gelatin to set," laments Margie, Mrs. Wilkes' daughter. "That's why this recipe, as well as others with a gelatin base, require canned, not fresh, pineapple."

1 (6-ounce) package lemon-flavored gelatin
1 cup boiling water
3 tablespoons sugar
1 cup light cream
1 cup chopped pecans
1 cup canned crushed pineapple, drained
1 (4-ounce) jar pimientos
1 (3-ounce) package cream cheese, softened

Place the gelatin in a large mixing bowl. Add the boiling water and sugar and stir until dissolved. Place the bowl in a refrigerator. When the gelatin is slightly congealed, add remaining ingredients. Stir gently until well blended. Pour into a lightly greased 6-cup mold. Refrigerate until ready to serve. Serves 6 to 8.

Fruit Coleslaw

1 large head cabbage, shredded
1 cup diced celery
2 cups white raisins
2 teaspoons sugar
3 apples, chopped
2 teaspoons lemon juice
1 cup mayonnaise
1 teaspoon curry powder (optional)
1 cup green seedless grapes

Combine the cabbage, celery, raisins, and sugar. Sprinkle the apples with the lemon juice and add to the coleslaw. When ready to serve, add the mayonnaise and curry. Pour into a serving dish and place grapes on top. Serves 8 to 10.
NOTE: For color, leave some peel on the apples.

Peach Nectar Salad

Luckily, peach nectar can be found today in food stores everywhere. This can also be made with apricot nectar and apricot-flavored gelatin or a combination of peach and apricot.

1 (3-ounce) package peach-flavored gelatin
1 (12-ounce) can peach nectar
1 (3-ounce) package cream cheese, softened and mashed
1 small can crushed pineapple with juice
1 cup pecans, chopped and lightly toasted
Lettuce
Mayonnaise
Mint or cherries

Dissolve the gelatin into hot, but not boiling, nectar. Add the cream cheese to the hot nectar. It will not be completely smooth, but a little lumpy. Add the pineapple and pecans. Pour into individual molds that have been sprayed with vegetable-oil cooking spray. Refrigerate until firm. To serve, unmold onto lettuce and top with a dollop of mayonnaise and sprig of mint or cherry with stem. Serves 6 to 8.

Easy Tomato Aspic

A must at every Southern ladies' luncheon.

1 (6-ounce) package lemon-flavored gelatin
1 cup boiling water
1 (16-ounce) can vegetable juice, chilled
2 tablespoons Worcestershire sauce
1 cup stuffed olives, sliced, plus extra for garnish
Lettuce

Dissolve the gelatin in the boiling water. Add the vegetable juice, Worcestershire, and olives and mix. Pour into a mold or oblong dish. When congealed, cut into squares. Place on a lettuce leaf and top with your favorite dressing. Garnish with additional olives. Serves 10 to 12.

"If you want my opinion, our whole society would be better off living in boarding houses.
"I mean even families, even married couples. Everyone should have his single room with a door that locks, and then a larger room downstairs where people can mingle or not as they please."

—Anne Tyler,
Celestial Navigation

Bean Salad

2 cups cooked or 1 (16-ounce) can French-cut green beans
1 cup cooked or 1 (8-ounce) can tiny English peas
2 stalks celery, cut into thin slices
1 large onion, thinly sliced
1 small bell pepper, diced
1 (4-ounce) jar chopped pimientos
1/2 cup salad oil
1 1/2 cups sugar
1 cup cider vinegar
1/2 cup water

Combine the beans, peas, celery, onion, bell pepper, and pimientos. In a separate bowl, combine the oil, sugar, vinegar, and water and mix until the sugar is dissolved. Pour over the vegetables. The salad will keep refrigerated for several days. Serves 6.

Chicken Salad with Fruit and Nuts

"For a pretty presentation, serve on a lettuce-lined plate—a refreshing cold meal," advises Marcia.

3 to 4 boneless, skinless chicken breasts
White wine
1/2 cup dairy sour cream
1/2 cup mayonnaise
1 cup chopped celery
1 cup green seedless grapes, cut in half
1 (11-ounce) can mandarin oranges, drained
1 cup toasted almonds, sliced or slivered
Salt and pepper

Place the chicken breasts in a 13 by 9-inch baking dish, fill with enough white wine to cover the breasts halfway, and marinate for 12 hours. Preheat the oven to 350°. Place the chicken in the oven and bake for 20 to 30 minutes, or until the chicken is tender and white all the way through. Cool, then cut into bite-sized pieces. Combine the sour cream and mayonnaise. Add the celery, grapes, oranges, and almonds, and season with salt and pepper to taste. Chill before serving. Serves 10 to 12.

Mrs. Wilkes Goes Global

Mrs. Wilkes is a Georgia gal, born and bred, not prone to straying too far from home. Most weekdays, you can find her working the dining room floor at 107 West Jones Street. But in the past few years, she has ventured a bit farther afield, serving as an unofficial emissary for the country cooking of her native Southland.

In 1986, she was invited to cook at Belvedere Castle in Belgium. She agreed to go only if her daughter, Margie, and granddaughter, Marcia, could join her. The three women lugged most of the ingredients across the Atlantic, but not the chickens. "Those Belgian chickens were the scrawniest little things we'd ever seen," recalls Marcia.

In 1989, Mrs. Wilkes traveled to Tokyo, Japan, where the New Otani Hotel was hosting the Georgia Food Fair. In preparation, the hotel sent one of its chefs, Yoshinao Nagumo, to study with Mrs. Wilkes in Savannah. "He had an awful hard time with pinches and dashes," remembers Mrs. Wilkes. "He wanted everything to be a science."

—J.T.E.

MENU FROM THE GEORGIA FOOD FAIR, 1989.

Soup

Ⓐ 野菜とパスタ入りクリームスープ ········· ¥600
Creamy Pasta Soup

Ⓑ ジョージア風挽肉入りスープ ········· ¥700
Brunswick Soup

Main Dish

Ⓒ リブ アイ ステーキ コロニアル風 ········· ¥3,300
Colonial Rib Eye Steak　　　　　　　(セット ¥4,100)

Ⓓ オイスター香味焼 ········· ¥1,800
Baked Oysters　　　　　　　(セット ¥2,600)

Ⓔ 南部好み オイスターバーガー ········· ¥1,400
Oyster Burger with Tartar Sauce　　　(セット ¥2,200)

Ⓕ 虹鱒ソテー サバナースペシャル ········· ¥1,700
Savannah Rainbow Trout Special　　　(セット ¥2,500)

Ⓖ 取り合せ野菜 "田舎風" ········· ¥1,200
Southern Vegetables　　　　　　　(セット ¥2,000)

Ⓗ 帆立貝の銀串焼 白ごま風味 ········· ¥2,200
Skewered Sesame Scallops　　　　　(セット ¥3,000)

Ⓘ アメリカン ヘルシー サラダ ········· ¥1,600
Healthy Delight Salad　　　　　　　(セット ¥2,400)

Ⓙ シーフード スパゲッティー ボーディングハウス ····· ¥1,700
Boarding House Seafood Spaghetti　　(セット ¥2,500)

Ⓚ ウィルクスおばさんのハンバーグステーキ ····· ¥1,800
Mrs. Wilkes' Hamburger Steak　　　　(セット ¥2,600)

※サービス料はいただいておりません。一部の料金には消費税をいただいております。
A 10% service charge will be added.

Set Menu

セットメニュー
セットには、
スープ、サラダ、パンと
コーヒーが付きます。

If you order a set course, soup, salad,
bread and coffee will be served with
the main dish.
《セットメニューの例》

SHRIMP SALAD

I 1/2 pounds cleaned and cooked shrimp
I cup sliced celery
1/2 cup chopped sweet pickles or pickle relish
I/4 cup sliced stuffed olives
I/2 cup mayonnaise
I/4 cup French dressing
Salt
Lemon juice
I/2 teaspoon minced onion (optional)

Cut the shrimp into bite-sized pieces. Combine with the remaining ingredients, including salt and lemon juice to taste, in a medium mixing bowl. Stir until well blended. Chill until ready to serve. Serves 4 to 6.

ORANGE SALAD

This refreshing fruity salad is particularly popular in the hot summer months.

I (6-ounce) package orange-flavored gelatin
I/2 cup sugar
I cup boiling water
I (8-ounce) can crushed pineapple, drained
I cup nuts, chopped
I (8-ounce) can mandarin oranges, drained
I cup dairy sour cream

Add the gelatin and sugar to the water and stir until dissolved. Add the pineapple, nuts, oranges, and sour cream. Pour into a lightly greased 6-cup mold, and chill until firm. Serves 4 to 6.

FIVE CUP SALAD

As easy to make as it is to remember—children like to help with this one!

I cup dairy sour cream
I cup shredded coconut

1 cup miniature marshmallows
1 (8-ounce) can mandarin oranges, drained
1 (8-ounce) can sliced pineapple, drained

Combine the sour cream, coconut, and marshmallows. Fold in the oranges and pineapple, and mix well. Allow to set in the refrigerator for several hours before serving. Serves 6 to 8.

CARROT SALAD

4 cups shredded carrots
1/2 cup raisins
1 cup finely chopped fresh pineapple
1/4 cup sugar
1/2 cup mayonnaise

Combine the carrots, raisins, pineapple, and sugar. Stir in the mayonnaise just before serving. If desired, add more mayonnaise if the salad appears too dry. Serves 6.
NOTE: For extra zest, add 2 tablespoons frozen orange juice concentrate.

BROCCOLI SALAD

3 cups chopped fresh broccoli
1 small red onion, chopped
8 strips bacon, cooked until crispy and crumbled
1/2 cup raisins
1/2 cup vinegar
1/4 cup flour
2 tablespoons prepared mustard
1 1/2 cups sugar
1 1/2 cups water
1 cup mayonnaise

Combine the broccoli, onion, bacon, and raisins. Combine the vinegar, flour, mustard, sugar, and water in a small saucepan and bring to a boil. Cook for 1 minute. Remove from the heat, add the mayonnaise, and allow to cool. Pour the mixture over the salad. Chill and serve. Serves 6.

Cucumber Mold or Salad

1 small (3-ounce) package lime-flavored gelatin
3/4 cup boiling water
1 cup mayonnaise
1 large unpeeled cucumber, grated (about 1 cup)
1 teaspoon onion powder

Dissolve the gelatin in hot water. Add the mayonnaise, cucumber, and onion powder. Pour into a mold or 8 by 8-inch dish. Chill until firm. Serves 6 to 8.

Vegetable Salad

1 medium head cauliflower, sliced
2 stalks celery, chopped
1 medium bell pepper, chopped
1 small (4-ounce) jar pimientos, drained
3/4 cup stuffed green olives
1/2 cup cubed Cheddar cheese
1 cup dairy sour cream
3 tablespoons olive juice
1 cup oil and vinegar dressing or dressing of your choice

Combine all of the ingredients and chill for several hours or overnight. Serves 4 to 6.

Copper Carrots

One of Margie's favorites, this vegetable dish is a wonderful accompaniment to fish and fowl.

2 pounds carrots, cleaned and sliced into rounds
1 (10 3/4-ounce) can condensed tomato soup
1/2 cup salad oil
3/4 cup vinegar
1 cup sugar
1 teaspoon dry mustard
1 teaspoon Worcestershire sauce
1/4 teaspoon salt
1/4 teaspoon pepper

1 small green pepper, chopped
1 medium onion, chopped
Hot sauce (optional)

Boil the carrots in salted water until they are just barely tender. Drain and cool. Combine the tomato soup, oil, vinegar, sugar, mustard, Worcestershire, salt, and pepper. Heat until the sugar is dissolved. In a bowl, alternate layers of carrots, peppers, and onion. Pour hot sauce over all and marinate for 24 hours in the refrigerator. Serve cold. This salad will keep for 2 weeks in the refrigerator. Serves 15.

Congealed Strawberry Salad

1 (6-ounce) package strawberry-flavored gelatin
2 cups boiling water
1 1/4 cups sliced fresh or 1 (10-ounce) package frozen
  strawberries
2 large bananas, mashed
1 cup pecans
1 (20-ounce) can crushed pineapple, drained
1 cup dairy sour cream

Dissolve the gelatin in the hot water. Add the strawberries. bananas, pecans, and pineapple and mix. Pour half into a 9 by 9-inch dish. Chill until firm. Spread the sour cream over the firm half, then pour the remaining half over it and chill until firm. Serves 6 to 8.

Apple Salad

4 cups pared, cored, and cubed Red Delicious apples
1/2 cup raisins
1 cup finely chopped fresh pineapple
1/2 cup miniature marshmallows
1/4 cup sugar
3/4 cup mayonnaise

Combine the apples. raisins, pineapple, marshmallows, and sugar. Stir in the mayonnaise just before serving. Serves 6 to 8.

"Those old ladies didn't play. They didn't use artificial anything. If you wanted flavor, you threw in some fatback."

—Cecilia Maxwell

POTATO SALAD, FAMILY STYLE

6 cups cubed, cooked potatoes
1/2 cup diced celery
3/4 cup chopped sweet pickles
1/2 cup chopped pimiento
2 tablespoons minced onion (optional)
4 hard-boiled eggs, chopped
1 1/2 teaspoons salt
1/4 teaspoon pepper
1 teaspoon prepared mustard
1 tablespoon vinegar or lemon juice
1/2 cup diced bell pepper
1 cup mayonnaise
Paprika

Place the potatoes, celery, pickles, pimiento, onion, eggs, salt, pepper, and mustard, vinegar, and bell pepper in a mixing bowl. Stir in the mayonnaise well, but lightly, with a wooden spoon. Pour into a serving dish, sprinkle with paprika, and add more pepper, if desired. Serves about 12.

TOMATO SALAD

2 pounds ripe tomatoes, peeled and diced
1 bunch green onions, chopped, including some of
  the whites
Salt
1/2 cup blue cheese dressing

Place the tomatoes in a covered dish. Add the green onions. Sprinkle with salt to taste. Pour the blue cheese dressing over the tomatoes and refrigerate. Drain. Serves 4.
NOTE: You can substitute ripe olives or pimiento-stuffed Spanish olives for the onions.

POTATO SALAD, FAMILY STYLE

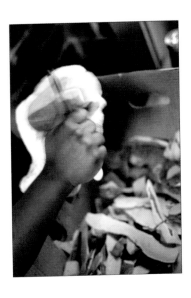

LAYERED GREEN SALAD

1 medium head iceberg lettuce, broken into pieces
1 cup chopped cucumbers, celery, or green pepper
1/2 cup minced mild onion
1 1/4 cups cooked green peas, 1 (10-ounce) package frozen
    green peas, cooked, or 1 (16-ounce) can peas, drained
2 cups mayonnaise
1/2 cup grated Parmesan or Cheddar cheese
1/2 pound bacon, fried to a crisp and crumbled
Tomatoes, peeled and cut into wedges (optional)

In a large, clear salad bowl, layer the ingredients in the above order. Do not toss the salad. Cover with plastic wrap and refrigerate for several hours before serving. Put tomato wedges on top just before serving. Serves 12.

MACARONI SALAD

Since the early '80s, regular diners at Mrs. Wilkes' have looked for this perennial favorite every Thursday.

1 (16-ounce) box elbow macaroni
2 hardboiled eggs, chopped
1 small cucumber, pared and finely chopped
6 green onions, finely sliced
1 tomato, diced
1 tablespoon prepared mustard
1 cup mayonnaise
1/2 teaspoon pepper

Cook the macaroni in salted water according to package's directions. Drain and rinse to remove starch. In a large mixing bowl, combine the macaroni with the eggs, cucumber, onions, and tomato and toss to mix well. Stir in the mustard, mayonnaise, and pepper. Chill until ready to serve. Serves 8.

Main Dishes

Life in the Kitchen

DAILY SPECIALS ARE POSTED AT
THE BACK DOOR.

Few restaurants in America can claim four generations of family stewardship. That continuity, that sense of purpose and pride, defines Mrs. Wilkes'. But to tell the story of this venerable Savannah restaurant—and tell it well—is to share the history of not one extended family but many, for the Wilkes, Martin, and Thompson families have long enjoyed the service of a strong cadre of black women, among them Lessie Bates, Mildred Capers, Denise Coleman, Mrs. Dempsey, Virginia Foster, Laverne Gould, Cassandra Johnson, Susie Mae Kennell, Florrie Simpson Leach, Cecilia Maxwell, Rose Marie Mobley, Millie Parrish, Exedene Walker, Linda Wright, and a host of others whose names have been lost to the years but whose indomitable spirits shine bright in the recollections of all.

To be sure, Mrs. Wilkes has always ruled the roost, and until not too long ago, you could find her in the kitchen each and every day. But the tasks of frying chicken, punching out biscuit dough, stripping collard leaves, and peeling potatoes have long been assigned to black women. In the kitchen, black arms flex to heft skillets to the stovetop; black backs bend to pull casseroles from the oven; black feet tread the kitchen duckboards from morning until night; black mouths taste for seasoning and add a dash more red pepper here, another pat of butter there. Always have, always will.

Since the first Dutch ship with twenty Africans for sale docked at Jamestown in 1619, we Southerners have been locked in a long and fitful dance of disharmony. For better than four centuries upon this North American continent, we have reaped the whirlwind of what has been euphemistically referred to as the "peculiar institution." There is much to regret, many wounds still to heal. And yet, in the kitchens south of the Mason-Dixon divide, there has always been a camaraderie unsuspected, a bond between black and white that confounds logic and spans generations. Young and old, rich and poor, we Southerners are united in our love of good food and our respect for those cooks whose hands have been ever on the Southern skillet. In the kitchen we talk and taste, celebrating a bond forged over countless kettles of black-eyed peas, untold pans of corn bread.

FLORRIE SIMPSON LEACH HAS WORKED HER DAILY MAGIC IN MRS. WILKES' KITCHEN FOR DECADES.

And so it has been for the Wilkes family since that day in the summer of 1942, when Sema Wilkes first agreed to lend a hand to her landlord, Mrs. Dennis Dixon. "There was a black lady already here in the kitchen when I showed up," recalls Mrs. Wilkes. "She was about the only one that stayed on when I took over for good in '43. She didn't stay with me that long, but she did help out. We've always had good help in the kitchen."

In Mrs. Wilkes' kitchen, cooks are known by their specialty. Twenty years ago, on one of the many occasions when Mrs. Wilkes was asked to share the secret to her success, she replied, "I've had the same chicken lady for more than twenty-five years, and my bread lady just a few months less." Put another way, there is no replacement for an experienced kitchen staff. The chicken lady of whom Mrs. Wilkes spoke was Mildred Capers. The bread lady was Susie Mae Kennell. Both retired in the 1980s and passed away not too long after. Along with Exedene Walker and boardinghouse maid Lessie Bates, they are remembered as the grand old women of Mrs. Wilkes' Boardinghouse.

Cassandra Johnson, a veteran of nearly twenty years at the stove, remembers Mildred the chicken cook well: "She taught me to beat that extra flour off the chicken and to listen for the sound of the oil in the fryer. When it dies down from a roar, when it gets quieter and the drumsticks start to float, well that's when it's near about ready. I watched her close. We taught one another, and Mrs. Wilkes was always there, too. In that kitchen we're a family. We squeeze by one another carrying pots and pans. We get in a hurry, but we always say, 'Excuse me,' and, 'Thank you.' And we always give praise to the Lord."

As for Susie Mae Kennell, she may well be the grande dame of them all. "I remember being covered in flour, playing with the dough as Susie patted out biscuits," says Emily Thompson, the great-granddaughter of Mrs. Wilkes. Ronnie Thompson— Emily's father and the long-serving de facto kitchen manager—also remembers Kennell well. "She was a force of nature in that kitchen," recalls Ronnie. "She never bit her tongue. She did things her way, no matter what you told her. I guess that was okay because she always did things well. But, man, could she ever slap out some biscuits! She had a certain way of rolling out the biscuits, of patting them out with her hands. They were always perfect, always the same size and shape. She was so good at it that she could roll out biscuits in her sleep. Sometimes we literally had to wake her up, her head would be drooping so far down that it would almost be in the dough bowl. But it didn't matter if she was awake or asleep, she just made perfect biscuits. Back when Sue was doing the baking, we had people who would come in and swear that we were using frozen biscuits because they looked so uniform. She was a wonder."

COMRADES OF THE KITCHEN, VIRGINIA FOSTER, RONNIE THOMPSON, AND ROSE MARIE MOBLEY SHARE A LAUGH AFTER THE DAILY RUSH HOUR.

Among present kitchen staff, the older generation of cooks is revered, in large part for their heroic work ethic and breadth of knowledge. But there is no denying that some of the fondness with which they are remembered is in tribute to stories told of pratfalls long since past.

LINDA WRIGHT AND CUSTOMER AT THE BACK DOOR. TAKE-OUT ORDERS ARE PICKED UP FROM THE LANE.

Cecilia Maxwell began her career at Mrs. Wilkes' in 1980, "picking over the greens for worms and stripping them down." It was a time of transition, as a new generation of cooks stepped to the fore. Now Cecilia is one of the cornerstone cooks, the bright-faced woman that everyone in the kitchen knows as Mommy. "Those old ladies like Exedene Walker, they were something," she recalls. "Exedene, she was one of the cart ladies, one of the girls that wheeled the food out into the dining room. She trained us from the old school. She was real short and plump, real spirited. It seems like her wig was always on backwards. Come to think of it, all those old ladies wore wigs. It didn't matter how old they were, though, they got around. I can see them now walking around the kitchen, holding onto tables for balance. One day Exedene slipped and slid underneath the stove—I mean all the way underneath the stove. We were just laughing and screaming, but she didn't miss a beat, she just kept on stirring the mashed potatoes. Exedene and them were tough."

For old-line employees like Exedene and Susie Mae, Ronnie once ran a virtual bus service, shuttling cooks and cart ladies alike from home to work and back again five days a week. "In the mornings, Ronnie would bomp that horn and those old ladies would stick a wig on their head and come on out the door," recalls Cecilia. "Susie Mae always got the front seat. Everybody else would fuss, but she got it." Those days are no more. "Recently, we've helped some of the ladies buy cars," says Ronnie. "The deal was, I'll help you with a down payment on a car if you agree to carpool, to bring somebody else with you. I hoped that might get me a few extra minutes sleep in the morning. But you know, I kind of miss driving around with those old ladies in the station wagon."

Two long-term employees are remembered as much for their service to the family as for their work in the dining room. During the days when

Mrs. Wilkes still accepted borders, Lessie Bates was the upstairs maid. "Back then, children weren't allowed to go upstairs," recalls Marcia Thompson. "But Lessie would let me help her iron and she'd let me in places where I wasn't supposed to be. Then, we had what we called a barracks room, a hall closet-like space where they stored the trunks and stuff that boarders had left there for the last hundred years. To a little girl of ten or twelve, these trunks full of old letters were like treasure chests. I remember Lessie as being my really good friend. She passed away not long ago, back in February of 2000."

FLORRIE SIMPSON LEACH AND DENISE COLEMAN FLANK MARCIA.

Linda Wright, an employee since 1973, is the modern-day inheritor of Lessie's mantle of family service. "I raised up Ryon and Emily," she'll tell most anyone. "Their momma Marcia is like a big sister to me. And Mrs Wilkes, we've got the same birthday, June 23rd. This place is home; they're family, sure as my own. I work in the dining room too—I'm the one that introduces Mrs. Wilkes when it's time for the prayer. I wouldn't want to be anywhere else. You know it's hell working with a bunch of women. We fuss and fight, but when it's all over we love each other same as we did when we started the day."

And then there's Florrie Simpson Leach, a constant in the Wilkes' kitchen since the early 1950s. Always animated, Florrie's words trip from her mouth in a stream of Gullah patois. A tightly wound and wizened octogenarian, prone to staccato bursts of laughter, she may well be the longest serving employee in the history of Mrs. Wilkes' Boardinghouse. "She never has any time on her hands," says Ronnie. "She's going to stay busy all day and you can bet she's always going to be smiling, laughing, washing dishes from daylight 'til dark. Her love of hard work is inspiring." Ask Florrie about her remarkable career, her unmatched tenure, and she will shrug and tell you that hard work is all she knows: "I was raised up without a mama on a farm. We cropped beans and peas and hogs. I love working, I love my people. And I ain't gonna quit 'til I can't go no more."   —J. T. E.

FRIED CHICKEN

One diner's instructions on how to find Mrs. Wilkes': "Walk along West Jones Street until you smell fried chicken."

1 (2 1/2-pound) fryer, cut up
Salt and pepper
2 tablespoons evaporated milk
2 tablespoons water
All-purpose flour
Vegetable oil

Sprinkle the fryer with salt and pepper. Pour the milk and water over the fryer and marinate for about 10 minutes. Dip in a bowl of all-purpose flour. Shake off the excess flour. Heat oil to 300° and deep-fry (or heat oil to medium and panfry) the chicken. Make sure the chicken is covered with oil at all times. Fry until golden brown. Serves 4 to 6.
NOTE: This recipe can be used for pork chops.

BAKED CHICKEN

Proof-positive that we Southerners don't fry *all* of our birds, this is a backdoor favorite with the locals.

4 pounds cut-up chicken
1 tablespoon salt
1 teaspoon pepper
1 teaspoon paprika
1/3 cup vegetable oil
1/2 cup butter or margarine
1 medium onion, grated

Preheat the oven to 350°. Sprinkle the chicken with the salt, pepper, and paprika. Mix the oil, butter, and onion. Toss the chicken in the mixture. Place the pieces of chicken flat in a roasting pan and pour the mixture over the chicken. Seal with foil and bake on the bottom rack of the oven for 20 minutes. Remove from the oven, drain the drippings, and pour over the chicken. Leave the roaster open and place on the top rack of the oven. Cook for about 30 minutes, until brown and tender. Serves 6 to 8.
NOTE: This recipe can be used for pork chops.

FRIED CHICKEN

LARD, LARD!

Why do Southerners eat so much fried chicken? More importantly, why do we excel at frying chicken? Though one could argue that there are a multitude of reasons, you can't deny the distinct advantage of easy access to the frying medium. Put another way, our love of the pig and the lard extracted therefrom has long ensured a steady supply of the grease that, when heated to bur-bling, insures a crisp crust, juicy meat, and the slight porcine taste we all praise. Granted, most of us now fry in vegetable oil or something similar, but trapped within most every skillet is a memory of lard past.   —J. T. E.

It must be Thursday: Laverne Gould is preparing chicken and dumplings.

CHICKEN AND DUMPLINGS

On Thursdays, these are expertly made by longtime cook Laverne Gould.

2 1/2 pounds chicken, cut up and ready to cook
1 teaspoon salt
1 teaspoon pepper

Place the chicken in a saucepan and cover with water. Sprinkle with the salt and pepper. Boil over medium heat for 30 minutes. Pour off the broth and save for the dumplings (recipe follows). Serves 6 to 8.

DUMPLINGS

Granddaughter Marcia vividly remembers Mrs. Wilkes making these dumplings: "I can see her rolling them out paper thin, then slicing them with a big butcher knife and dropping them into her huge pots of roiling broth."

2 cups all-purpose flour
2 cups milk
1/2 cup water
Salt and pepper

Mix the flour, 1/2 cup of the milk, and the water in a bowl and knead until the dough is firm. Mash flat on a floured surface. Let stand for about 10 minutes. Roll out with a rolling pin until knife-blade thin and cut into 2-inch squares. Drop into boiling broth. Cook for about 10 minutes over high heat. Reduce the heat to low and return the chicken to the pot. Pour the remaining 1 1/2 cups milk into the mixture and stir. Remove from the heat. Season with salt and pepper to taste.

Baked Buttermilk Chicken

4 to 6 boneless, skinless chicken breasts
1 1/2 cups buttermilk
1/4 cup flour
1/2 teaspoon salt
1/4 teaspoon pepper
1/4 cup butter or margarine
1 (10 1/2-ounce) can cream of mushroom soup
Parsley, for garnish

Preheat the oven to 425°. Dip the chicken in 1/2 cup of the buttermilk, then roll the chicken in a mixture of flour, salt, and pepper. Melt the butter in a 9 by 13 by 2-inch pan. Place the chicken in the pan. Bake, uncovered, for 30 minutes. Turn the chicken and bake for 15 minutes more. Combine the remaining 1 cup buttermilk and soup. Pour over chicken and bake for 15 minutes more. Remove the chicken, place on a platter, and garnish with parsley. Serve with pan gravy. Serves 4 to 6.

Barbecue Chicken

A Thursday lunch favorite with folks who line up at the back door to take away Styrofoam containers piled high with Mrs. Wilkes' good cooking.

1/2 cup flour
1 (2-pound) fryer, cut into 4 parts
1/2 cup butter
Spicy Barbecue Sauce (page 43)

Flour the chicken lightly. Heat the butter and brown the chicken quickly. Heat the sauce and pour over the chicken. Simmer, covered, for about 40 minutes, until tender. Serves 4.

Chicken Cacciatore

In the early days, when diners were eating three meals a day at Mrs. Wilkes', meals like this provided diversity.

12 pieces mixed chicken (about 2 fryers, cut up)
1/4 cup oil
Flour for dredging
2 onions, chopped
1/2 green pepper, julienned
1/2 teaspoon garlic powder
2 bay leaves
1/2 teaspoon celery seed
3 or 4 tomatoes, chopped, or 1 (15-ounce) can tomato
    sauce
1/2 cup water
1/2 cup mushrooms, sliced
1 cup grated Cheddar cheese

Preheat the oven to 350°. Dip the chicken in flour. Heat the oil and cook the chicken on both sides until lightly browned. When the chicken is browned, transfer to a large casserole dish. Pour off all but 2 tablespoons of oil from skillet. Sauté the onions and peppers with the garlic powder until soft. Add the bay leaves, celery seed, tomatoes, water, and mushrooms. Bake for 1 hour. Sprinkle the cheese over the casserole about 15 minutes before removing from the oven. Serves 6 to 8.

Roast Beef

1 (3- to 4-pound) chuck roast
1 tablespoon salt
1 teaspoon pepper
1/2 teaspoon garlic powder
2 tablespoons Kitchen Bouquet
2 cups water

Preheat the oven to 350°. Sprinkle the roast with the salt, pepper, and garlic powder. Rub the Kitchen Bouquet over the roast. Place in a roaster with the water. Seal the top with foil. Bake on the bottom rack of the oven for 1 1/2 hours, or until tender. Use the drippings for gravy. Serves 10 to 12.

Sema Says

Ask Mrs. Wilkes how old she is, and she replies, "I don't even tell myself!"

"If collards are real dark, real green, well, they're tough and you're gonna have to cook them a while. But if they are light and have seeds on them, well, they're tender."

"They used to do all the prep work outdoors, sitting at a big old picnic table. When it was wet, they got up under the eaves of the house, and when it was cold, they wore mittens and coats."

"When you're fixing up the sweet potatoes, you can't be afraid of sugar. Don't let it scare you."

"For black-eyed peas, get you a ham skin, the cap of skin that you pull off the top of a ham. Throw that in the pot with the peas."

ROAST TURKEY

Cook Rose Marie Mobley is expert at roasting turkey. She and Mrs. Wilkes advise, "Treat a turkey just as you would a chicken." Two weeks before Thanksgiving and Christmas, roast turkey is a daily offering on the table at Mrs. Wilkes'.

1 (10- to 12-pound) turkey
Salt and black pepper
Paprika
1/2 cup melted butter or margarine
1/2 cup salad oil
Corn Bread Dressing (page 112)

If the turkey is frozen, thaw it in the refrigerator until ready to cook. Preheat the oven to 375°. Sprinkle the bird generously with salt, pepper, and paprika inside and out. Mix the butter and oil. Place the turkey in a roasting pan, breast side up, and pour the butter and oil mixture over it. Pour 4 cups water into the pan. Seal the pan with heavy foil. Bake for about 3 hours, or as directed on the wrapper. Turkeys vary, so after about 1 1/2 hours, open the roaster and baste with the stock in the pan to ensure tenderness. Reseal and return to the oven. When the turkey is tender, remove and drain, reserving the stock to use for the dressing. Add water to the stock if more liquid is needed for dressing. Drain the excess fat and save for the gravy. Serves 10.

PEPPER STEAK

Often served at night, in a bowl, to hungry boarders.

1 1/2 pounds round steak
Salt and pepper
Flour for dredging
Vegetable oil
1 (11-ounce) can onion soup
1 cup catsup
1 medium onion, chopped
1 cup water
1 medium bell pepper, chopped

Cut the steak into serving-sized pieces. Sprinkle with salt and pepper. Heat the oil. Dip the steak in flour and brown quickly in the oil. Add the soup, catsup, chopped onion, and water.

Simmer on low for 45 minutes or until the steak is tender. Add the bell pepper 15 minutes before removing from the heat. Serve over hot rice. Serves 4.

BEEF BOURGUIGNONNE

2 tablespoons vegetable oil
3 or 4 medium onions, sliced
1/2 pound fresh or 1 (3-ounce) can sliced mushrooms
1 (2-pound) round steak, cut into 1-inch pieces
1 teaspoon salt
1/4 teaspoon crushed marjoram
1/4 teaspoon crushed thyme
1/4 teaspoon pepper
1 1/2 tablespoons flour
3/4 cup beef bouillon (from 1 bouillon cube and 3/4 cup boiling water)
1 1/2 cups Burgundy wine

Heat the oil and cook the onions until tender. Add the mushrooms and cook until tender. Drain on paper towels. Brown the steak in the remaining oil in the pan. Remove from the heat and sprinkle the salt, marjoram, thyme, and pepper over the steak. Mix the flour and bouillon. Add to the skillet. Boil for 1 minute. Stir in the burgundy, reduce the heat to low, and cook for about 2 hours, covered. Take the lid off and gently stir in the onions and mushrooms. Cook, uncovered, for 15 minutes. Serves 6 to 8.

BEEF HASH

"Everyone, especially our boarders, hoped for this favorite leftover," relates Mrs. Wilkes.

Leftover roast, chipped
1 medium onion
Leftover beef gravy or broth

Preheat the oven to 350°. Place the roast in a small pan. Grate the onion over the roast. Add the gravy. If this is not enough liquid, add some water so it will not burn. Bake for about 30 minutes, until well heated and brown. Stir occasionally to brown through and through. Yield depends on amount of leftovers.

Pot Roast Beef

1 (5- to 6-pound) rump roast
Soy sauce
Black pepper
Water
Carrots, potatoes, or other root vegetables, washed,
    peeled, and coarsely chopped
2 tablespoons flour

Trim the fat from the roast. Sprinkle the roast generously with soy sauce and black pepper. (No salt is needed since there is salt in the soy sauce.) Place the roast in a pot and pour the soy sauce and water about 1-inch deep, using 3 parts soy sauce to 1 part water. Cover and cook on the stovetop for about 30 minutes per pound, or until fork tender. Use low heat and turn the roast occasionally so it will be nice and brown. About 30 minutes before the roast is done, add the carrots. When done, remove the vegetables and roast. The drippings left in the pot will make the most delicious gravy. Mix the flour in 1 cup water. Add to the drippings. Use a whisk to dissolve the lumps. Cook over low heat and stir; the mixture will thicken. Your vegetables will have a great flavor and will not need any salt. Serves 10 to 12.

Country-Style Steak

This is a favorite family tradition around the holidays, especially for Mrs. Wilkes' great-grandson Ryon. Mrs. Wilkes makes the steak crispy on the outside and tender on the inside. It is best served with white rice.

3 pounds cubed steak
Worcestershire sauce
Salt
Pepper
Pinch of garlic powder
Flour for dredging
1/4 cup vegetable oil
1/2 cup minced onion
3 1/4 cups hot water
3 tablespoons flour

Place the steak in a casserole dish and generously sprinkle with Worcestershire sauce. Cover and marinate overnight. Remove from the marinade and sprinkle generously with salt, pepper, and garlic powder. Dip the steak in flour and shake. Heat the oil and quickly fry the steak until brown, but do not cook the inside too much. This is done by cooking both sides on high heat, turning quickly, and then reducing heat to low to finish cooking.

FRESH MEATS AND SAUSAGES WERE PLENTIFUL FOR CUSTOMERS AT THE CITY MARKET. THIS PHOTO DATES FROM 1950.

Boil 1/2 cup minced onion in another pot with 1/4 cup of the water for about 5 minutes. When finished cooking as many steaks as desired, leave about 3 tablespoons browned crumbs (not burned) and drippings from steak in skillet. Add onion and 3 tablespoons flour. Stir until slightly browned. Slowly pour in the remaining 3 cups hot water as it thickens. Season with salt and pepper to taste. The gravy may be served over rice or steaks. Serves 6 to 8.

Sweet and Sour Meatballs

By omitting the rice or pasta, this becomes an appetizer.

1 pound ground chuck
1 cup catsup
1/3 cup brown sugar
1/2 cup water
1 teaspoon Worcestershire sauce
1/2 teaspoon dry mustard
1/2 teaspoon soy sauce

Roll the meat into small meatballs and sauté for 15 minutes. Pour off any fat. Combine the catsup, sugar, water, Worcestershire, mustard, and soy sauce and pour over the meatballs. Simmer for 15 to 20 minutes. Add more water if the sauce becomes too thick. Serve over rice or pasta. Serves 4.

MEAT LOAF

This comfort food can be found on the menu every Wednesday.

2 eggs
2 pounds ground chuck
2 cups cornflakes, crushed
3/4 cup minced onion
1/4 cup minced green pepper
2 tablespoons soy sauce
2 1/2 teaspoons salt
1/4 cup milk
1 (10 1/2-ounce) can cream of mushroom soup

Preheat the oven to 350°. Beat the eggs slightly with a fork. Lightly mix in the meat, cornflakes, onions, and pepper. Add the soy sauce, salt, milk, and soup. The secret is to mix well but lightly. Do not pack. Shape meat into an oval loaf in the baking dish. Bake for 50 minutes, or until done. Serves 6 to 8.

BEEF STEW CASSEROLE

2 pounds beef stew meat
1 teaspoon salt
Pinch of pepper
1/3 cup flour
2 tablespoons vegetable oil
1 large onion, quartered
1 cup apple juice
3 carrots, cut in long, narrow strips
1 cup (1/2-inch chunks) celery
2 medium-sized cooking apples, sliced
1 bay leaf
1/4 teaspoon oregano

Season the meat with the salt and pepper. Dredge in the flour. Heat the oil in a frying pan. Brown the meat and add the onion. Pour the apple juice over the meat; bring to a boil. Cover and simmer for about 1 1/2 hours, or until tender. Preheat the oven to 350°. Place the carrots, celery, and apples in a casserole dish and pour the stew on top. Add the bay leaf and oregano and bake for about 30 minutes. Serve over mashed potatoes or rice. Serves 6.

Sema Says

"The secret of meat loaf is to have good chuck ground to order. Then grate the ingredients that go into it. The cornflakes bind all the ingredients together."

Chop Suey

Believe it or not, this was a popular regular feature on the menu for many years. It is still a family favorite, especially with Beth Martin, Margie's sister-in-law.

1 pound round steak
1 pound pork ham
Salt
Pepper
Flour for dredging
Vegetable oil
1 stalk celery, chopped
3 medium onions, diced
1 (5-ounce) bottle soy sauce
2 (14-ounce) cans bean sprouts
2 tablespoons Chinese molasses

Cut the steak and ham into bite-sized pieces. Season with salt and pepper, dip in the flour, and brown in cooking oil. Add the celery, onion, soy sauce, and juice drained from the bean sprouts. Cook slowly for about 1 hour, stirring from time to time. Add the bean sprouts. Cook for about 20 minutes. Mix the molasses with enough flour to make a thick consistency and add to the vegetables. Serve on rice. Serves about 8.

Home-Style Barbecue Beef

1 1/2 pounds beef tips
Vegetable oil
1 (10-ounce) can tomato purée
1 cup water
1 cup Spicy Barbecue Sauce (page 43) or barbecue sauce of your choice

Preheat the oven to 350°. In a sauté pan, brown the beef tips lightly in a very small amount of vegetable oil. Drain the oil from the meat. Place the meat in a pan. Add the tomato purée and water. Pour the barbecue sauce over the meat and cover. Cover and bake in the oven, or on top of the stove in a Dutch oven, until tender. The juices will be very thick. Serves 6 to 8.

BEEF STEW

Potatoes and carrots are recent additions to the stew. "Things have changed along the way," says Margie Martin.

3 pounds boneless beef stew meat or short ribs
Salt and pepper
1 large onion, sliced
3 medium potatoes, cut into chunks
6 medium carrots, cut into chunks
2 tablespoons flour

Cut the meat into serving-sized portions and place in a heavy pot. Season each piece with salt and pepper. Add the onion and enough water to cover the bottom of pot. Cook, covered, over medium heat. When the meat is cooking well, remove the lid and allow the meat to cook in its juices. Turn the meat with a fork until brown. Add the potatoes and carrots. Cover and cook over low heat for about 1 hour. Check frequently; if the juices are cooking out, then add some water. When the meat is fork tender, add the flour to water and pour over the meat. Stir well. If the broth becomes too thick, add more water. Simmer until ready to serve. Serves 10 to 12.

CORNED BEEF AND CABBAGE

The second largest St. Patrick's Day parade in the country graces Savannah's streets, and the large Irish-descent population relishes Mrs. Wilkes' corned beef and cabbage.

1 pound corned beef
1 medium head cabbage, cut up
1 tablespoon butter or margarine
Salt

Cook the beef in a small amount of water over low heat for 1 hour, until tender. Slice it into small pieces. Add the cabbage to the broth; return the meat to the pot. Heat to a boil and cook for 5 minutes more. Add the butter and stir slightly to mix the beef and cabbage. Add salt to taste. Serves 4 to 6.

This is not a cookbook for purists. Mrs. Wilkes has long used the versatile canned cream of mushroom soup—a standard in Southern pantries since Campbell Soup Company introduced it in 1934, making it the first soup to be widely used as a sauce.

Chili

Carole Scott, a childhood friend of Marcia, recalls that she learned to cook from Mrs. Wilkes' *Famous Recipes*. "This," she says, "is a great no-fail recipe for newlyweds!"

2 pounds ground chuck
1 large onion, chopped
1 teaspoon garlic powder
1 teaspoon salt
1/4 teaspoon pepper
1 can tomato soup
3 fresh or 1 (16-ounce) can tomatoes
1 tablespoon Worcestershire sauce
1 3/4 cups cooked or 1 (16-ounce) can kidney beans
1 tablespoon chile powder

Brown the ground beef and onion in a skillet over medium-high heat. Add the remaining ingredients. Mix well. Bring to a boil, reduce to the lowest heat, and simmer, covered, for 1 hour. Serve with buttered saltines. Serves 8.

Roast Pork

This is a kissin' cousin to beef pot roast.

1 (4- to 5-pound) pork roast
1 teaspoon salt
1 teaspoon pepper
1 teaspoon paprika
2 cups water

Preheat the oven to 350°. Season the roast with the salt, pepper, and paprika. Place in a roaster and add the water. Seal the top with foil and bake for 1 1/2 hours, or until tender. Serves 10 to 12.

Baked Ham

Mrs. Wilkes remembers her father putting up his own hams and sausages in the smokehouse behind their house.

1 (10-pound) bone-in pit ham, cooked
1 small (10-ounce) jar pineapple preserves
Juice of 1 lemon
Pinch of ground cloves (optional)
1 (16-ounce) can pineapple slices
Maraschino cherries

Preheat the oven to 325°. Trim the excess fat and skin from the ham. Insert the meat thermometer in the thickest part of the ham (do not touch bone). Place in a shallow roasting pan and bake for 2 hours. Combine the preserves, lemon juice, and ground cloves and brush onto the ham. Garnish with pineapple and cherries. Return to the oven to bake until the thermometer reaches 140°. Serves 12 to 15.

Individual Ham Casseroles

1 egg, beaten
2 1/2 cups cooked corn bread, crumbled
1/4 cup water
2 tablespoons melted butter or margarine
1 cup frozen or canned mixed vegetables
1 small onion, grated
1 cup catsup (optional)
2 cups cooked and cubed ham
Grated sharp Cheddar cheese

Preheat the oven to 350°. Mix the egg, corn bread, water, and butter. Press the mixture into the bottom and sides of 6 lightly greased individual casserole dishes. Bake for 10 to 12 minutes. Cook the vegetables and onion in a small amount of boiling water until tender. Add the catsup and ham. Heat until bubbly and pour into the prepared dishes. Sprinkle with the cheese, return to the oven, and heat until the cheese is melted. Serves 6.

Barbecue Pork

When you're in a pinch and can't stoke the pit with hickory or oak, try this simple preparation, which people clamor for at Mrs. Wilkes'.

Roast Pork (page 90)
Spicy Barbecue Sauce (page 43)

Preheat the oven to 300°. When the pork is tender, let it cool and then slice. Generously cover the pork with the barbecue sauce and return it to the oven. Bake, uncovered, for about 30 minutes. Serves 10 to 12.

Spareribs and Sauerkraut

3 pounds spareribs
2 to 4 tablespoons salad oil
2 large onions, minced
1/4 teaspoon salt
Pepper
1/2 cup boiling water
1 (14-ounce) can sauerkraut
1/4 to 1/2 teaspoon caraway seeds
1 apple, grated (optional)
1/8 teaspoon pepper

In a Dutch oven sauté the spareribs in hot oil until brown on all sides. Add the onions and cook until tender. Sprinkle with the salt and pepper. Add the water and simmer, covered, for 1 hour. Add the sauerkraut, caraway seeds, and apple. Cook, covered, for 20 to 30 minutes. Season to taste. Serves 4.

Venison Roast

When they're lucky enough to have it, many people puzzle over how to prepare venison. Here's a great reliable solution.

1 (4-pound) venison ham
Salt and pepper
Mint jelly
Suet (the butcher will give you this)

1 cup chopped pecans
1 cup chopped apples

Preheat the oven to 350°. Generously season the ham with salt and pepper. Make a cavity in the meat and rub it inside and out with mint jelly. Place the pecans and apples inside the cavity. Cover with the suet (fat cut from beef) and tie the ham well with string. Place the ham in a pan and seal with foil. Bake for about 2 hours. Remove from the oven. Use drippings with nuts and apples for gravy. Serve with rice. Serves 8 to 10.

CRAB QUICHE

Great for brunch, served with a tossed salad and fresh fruit.

1/2 cup mayonnaise
2 tablespoons flour
2 eggs, beaten
1/2 cup milk
1 cup crabmeat
1/2 cup grated Cheddar cheese
1/2 cup chopped onion
1 Standard Piecrust (page 163) or other unbaked piecrust

Preheat the oven to 350°. Combine the mayonnaise, flour, eggs, and milk and mix well. Stir in the crab, cheese, and onion. Pour into the piecrust and bake for 45 minutes. Serves 8.
NOTE: You can substitute other meats such as tuna, chopped ham, cubed chicken, or shrimp.

BAKED FLOUNDER

4 (4- to 5-ounce) flounder or other whitefish fillets
Salt and pepper
1/4 cup chopped green pepper
1/4 cup minced onion
1 (6-ounce) can tomato juice
Grated Parmesan cheese

Preheat the oven to 450°. Season each fillet with salt and pepper. Place the fillets on a buttered baking dish. Sprinkle the green peppers and onion over the fish. Pour the tomato juice over the fish and bake for 30 minutes. Sprinkle the cheese on top and serve at once. Serves 4.

MONDAY'S
BLACKBOARD
MENU

Fried Chicken

Beef Stew

Sausage

Baked Ham

Cabbage

Snap Beans

Black-Eyed Peas

Rutabaga

Squash

Rice and Gravy

Mashed Potatoes

Candied Yams

Pickled Beets

Red Rice

Okra and Tomatoes

BETH'S SEAFOOD CASSEROLE

Margie's sister-in-law, Beth Martin, introduced this recipe, and it has been a family favorite at reunions ever since.

1/2 cup butter or margarine
1/2 cup chopped green pepper
1/2 cup finely chopped onion
1 cup chopped celery
1/2 cup chopped pimiento
1 (10 1/2-ounce) can cream of mushroom soup
1/2 cup or 1 (4-ounce) can sliced mushrooms (optional)
1 cup mayonnaise
1/2 teaspoon salt
1/2 teaspoon pepper
1 tablespoon lemon juice
1 tablespoon Worcestershire sauce
1 cup milk
3 cups cooked rice
1 pound claw crabmeat
1 pound cooked shrimp
1/4 pound grated mild Cheddar cheese

Preheat the oven to 350°. Heat the butter and sauté the green pepper, onion, and celery. Add the pimiento, mushroom soup, mushrooms, mayonnaise, salt, pepper, lemon juice, Worcestershire, milk, rice, crab, and shrimp and mix. Pour the mixture into a 3-quart casserole and top with the cheese. Bake for 45 minutes. This is great for a family dinner or covered dish supper. Serves 8 to 10.

Baked Mullet

Mr. Martin's brother-in-law, Norman Grosser of Jacksonville, Florida, loved to cast his nets into St. John's River and bring home mullet to be prepared just this way.

2 pounds mullet fillets
1/2 cup French dressing
1 1/2 cups crushed cheese crackers
2 tablespoons vegetable oil
Paprika

Preheat the oven to 500°. Skin the fillets and cut them into serving-sized portions. Dip the fillets in the dressing and roll them in the cracker crumbs. Place on a well-greased shallow pan or cookie sheet. Drizzle the oil over the fish. Sprinkle with paprika. Bake for 10 to 12 minutes, or until the fish flakes easily with a fork. Serves 6.

Baked Oysters

Oysters are always popular in Savannah, and this recipe is a favorite holiday dish for the Wilkes family.

1 quart shucked oysters
2 cups cooked spinach, chopped
1/4 cup chopped onion
2 bay leaves
1 tablespoon chopped parsley
1/3 cup butter or margarine
1/2 teaspoon celery salt
8 drops Tabasco sauce
1/2 cup cornflake crumbs

Preheat the oven to 400°. Wash and drain the oysters. Spread out the oysters and place them in a well-greased shallow pan. Mix the spinach, onion, bay leaves, and parsley well, then cook the mixture in butter for about 5 minutes. Add the celery salt and Tabasco. Stir the crumbs into the mixture with a fork. Sprinkle the mixture over the oysters and bake for about 10 minutes. Serves 4 to 6.

CURRIED SHRIMP

"We were introduced to this especially memorable main dish for company by our dear family friend 'Duck' Huey," relates Marcia.

2 cups boiled shrimp, salted
1 (10 1/2-ounce) can cream of celery soup
1 teaspoon curry powder
1 3/4 cups cooked or 1 (16-ounce) can small English peas,
    drained
1 pint dairy sour cream

Heat the shrimp in celery soup. Add the curry powder and peas. Cook over low heat, just until the mixture begins to bubble. Remove from the heat and stir in the sour cream until well blended. Season with salt and pepper to taste. Serve over hot rice with tossed salad. Serves 4.

SHALLOW FRIED FISH

Owing to the large Roman Catholic population in Savannah, fried fish used to be a standard on Fridays. Vatican II and the demand for fried chicken preempted it.

1 to 1 1/2 pounds flounder or other small fish fillets
Salt and pepper
2/3 cup cornmeal
1/3 cup flour
Cooking oil

Generously season the flounder with salt and pepper on both sides. Combine the cornmeal and flour and dip the fish into the mixture. In a deep skillet, heat 1 1/2 inches oil to about 370°. Immerse the fish in the hot oil and fry quickly until browned on both sides. The fillets should be flaky but moist. This will take about 3 or 4 minutes, depending on the size of the fillets. Drain on paper towels. Serve immediately. Serves 4.

Salmon Croquettes

Mrs. Wilkes served these regularly on Friday nights throughout the '50s. Don't try this with fresh salmon, however—it would be a waste.

1 (16-ounce) can red salmon, drained
2 eggs
1 tablespoon grated onion
1 teaspoon black pepper
1/2 cup cornflake crumbs
1 medium cooked potato, diced
Vegetable oil

Combine all of the ingredients and mix well but lightly. Form into small egg-shaped patties. Fill a pan 1/4-inch deep with oil, heat, and fry the patties for 7 or 8 minutes, or until golden brown. Serves 4.

Skillet-Fried Oysters

3 tablespoons butter or margarine
3 tablespoons vegetable oil
2 dozen shucked large raw oysters, drained
2 eggs, beaten
3 cups cracker crumbs
3/4 to 1 teaspoon salt
1/4 teaspoon pepper
Snipped parsley or paprika
Lemon wedges

Heat the butter and oil in a skillet. Roll the oysters in the egg and crackers crumbs and sprinkle with salt and pepper. Sauté the oysters, turning once, until golden brown. Sprinkle the parsley or paprika on top and garnish with lemon. Serves 4.

City Market

Jim D. Mathews, Sr., has eaten at Mrs. Wilkes' for over 43 years. His father was Frank C. Mathews, Sr., the owner of a seafood retail and wholesale business in the old City Market and later at 116 West Congress Street. Mathews remembers that Mrs. Wilkes would arrive early in the morning to inspect each and every fish she purchased for quality and freshness. "Mrs. Wilkes would open the gills and check them for red freshness and feel their stomachs for lack of firmness," recalls Mr. Mathews. "As a youth it was my job from time to time to deliver Mrs. Wilkes' order to Jones Street. She would reinspect the fish, having left them for us to remove the scales and clean per her instructions. And she could tell you, 'Yes, there are thirty-eight fish here, but I did not buy this one. You can take it back and tell Mr. Frank he owes me one'"

No Savannah cookbook is complete without a variation of the local favorite, crab cakes. Be sure to make plenty—most dinner guests will want seconds!

DEVILED CRAB

Deviled crabs are a Low Country favorite. If you don't have the whole crab to stuff this preparation in, ramekins or little baking tins will fill the bill.

1 medium bell pepper, chopped
1 medium onion, chopped
1 medium stalk celery, chopped
1 to 2 tablespoons cooking oil
1 pound crabmeat, washed and picked over for shell
1/2 cup bread crumbs
1 tablespoon prepared mustard
1 tablespoon catsup
1 tablespoon mayonnaise
Crab shells

Preheat the oven to 400°. Brown the bell pepper, onion, and celery in 1 or 2 tablespoons oil. Combine with the remaining ingredients in a bowl and mix well. Place in crab shells and bake for 20 minutes. Serves 4 to 6.

CRAB CAKES

3 cups crabmeat, washed and picked over for shell
1 1/2 teaspoons salt
1 teaspoon dry mustard
1/2 teaspoon pepper
1 egg yolk
2 teaspoons Worcestershire sauce
1 tablespoon mayonnaise
1 egg, slightly beaten
2 tablespoons water
Flour
2 cups bread crumbs
Salad oil, butter, or margarine

Combine the crabmeat, salt, mustard, pepper, egg yolk, Worcestershire, and mayonnaise. Form the mixture into small cakes. Beat the egg and water in a small bowl. Dip the cakes into the flour, then the egg mixture, then the crumbs. Brown quickly in oil over high heat. Serves 4 to 6.

Sema Says

"I always say, never have too many spices in one dish."

AT ANY GIVEN LUNCH, MORE THAN FIFTY
PLATTERS OF CHICKEN ARE SERVED.

CRAB DINNER

I pound crabmeat, washed and picked over for shell
1/2 cup cooked tiny English peas
I (10 1/2-ounce) can cream of mushroom soup
Pepper
6 crab shells
1/2 cup grated Cheddar cheese
Paprika

Preheat the oven to 350°. Combine the crab, peas, soup, and pepper. Divide the mixture into shells. Sprinkle with the cheese and paprika. Bake for 20 to 25 minutes, or until brown. Serves 6.

SHRIMP AND CRAB CASSEROLE

4 tablespoons butter or margarine
4 tablespoons flour
1/2 teaspoon salt
1/4 teaspoon pepper
1/8 teaspoon Tabasco sauce
2 cups milk
I 1/2 cups grated Cheddar cheese
8 ounces cooked shrimp
4 ounces crabmeat, washed and picked over for shell

Preheat the oven to 350°. Melt the butter in a large saucepan. Add the flour, salt, pepper, and Tabasco and stir until well blended. Add the milk, stirring constantly until smooth. Stir in 1/2 cup of the cheese. Add the shrimp and crab and continue stirring until well mixed. Pour into a 1-quart baking dish and sprinkle the remaining 1 cup cheese on top. Bake for 20 minutes. Serves 4.

Shrimp Creole

"This is my own Friday-night favorite," says Margie Martin.

1/4 cup butter or margarine
1 large onion, chopped
1/2 cup minced green peppers
1 minced clove garlic, or 1 teaspoon garlic powder
1 teaspoon salt
Pinch of pepper
1/8 teaspoon dried rosemary
1/8 teaspoon paprika
2 cups cooked or canned tomatoes
1 pound cooked, cleaned shrimp
2 to 3 cups hot cooked rice

Melt the butter in a saucepan. Add the onion, green pepper, garlic, salt, pepper, rosemary, and paprika. Sauté for 10 minutes, or until tender. Add the tomatoes. Bring to a boil; reduce the heat and simmer for 15 minutes. Add the shrimp and heat thoroughly. Serve on hot, fluffy rice. Serves 4.

Baked Pork Chops

The secret to Mrs. Wilkes' tender, flavorful chops lies in her use of Worcestershire and soy sauces and lemon juice.

6 (3/4-inch-thick) pork chops
2 tablespoons catsup
1 tablespoon Worcestershire sauce
2 tablespoons cooking oil
1 tablespoon lemon juice
1 tablespoon soy sauce

Preheat the oven to 350°. Place the chops in a baking dish. Whisk or beat the remaining ingredients in a small bowl. Spread half of the mixture over the chops. Bake, uncovered, for 30 minutes. Turn the chops and spread the remaining mixture on the other side. Bake, uncovered, for 30 minutes more. Serves 6.

Vegetables

The View from the Lane

Mrs. Wilkes' is a democratic institution of the highest order. No matter your social rank or status on the silver screen, if you arrive between the hours of, say, 11:30 and 2:30, you will wait in line to be seated. Indeed, most diners at Mrs. Wilkes' spend a good thirty minutes out front cooling their heels on the brick sidewalk.

But a host of regulars—truck drivers on their weekly run from Jacksonville, Florida to Buffalo, New York; registered nurses with fifteen minutes of breathing time between shifts; and longtime Wilkes family friends among them—have a different idea. They get their food to go at a take-out door facing on the rear alley, a thoroughfare known hereabouts as the lane.

It's not a secret. Anyone can abandon his spot in line, ease down the passageway on the west side of the building, and thread his way through the kitchen crew seated out back on overturned plastic buckets, slicing summer squash into delicate sunshine-yellow rounds and stripping collards leaf by leaf. That said, most backdoor devotees arrive from the rear, by way of the lane.

JONES LANE, CIRCA 1900.

Ever wonder whether the cooks at Mrs. Wilkes' Boardinghouse still use fresh ears of Silver Queen for that creamed corn? Well, just take a look at that spent croaker sack over in the corner, stuffed full of raggedy, green husks. They can't possibly peel whole sweet potatoes for those candied yams, now, can they? Tell that to Rose Marie Mobley, who sits crouched, with her back to the brick wall, slicing one orange tuber after another. You can learn a lot by sidling up to the back door.

More than likely, Denise Coleman will be standing at the threshold, a typhoon of coarse black hair spiraling upward from her head, at the ready to fill your order. Above her, an old box fan is fixed to the door jamb, slapping out a rickety beat as it turns round and round, stirring the sweet scents that swirl up and out and over the lane each time the oven door swings wide. To her left, on a bleached-out chalkboard, are scrawled the daily specials. Monday it's red rice; Tuesday it's chicken and dressing. On Wednesday macaroni and cheese debuts; Thursday it's barbecue chicken. Friday signals the arrival of English peas. Day in, day out, massive kettles of okra and tomatoes, black-eyed peas, snap beans, and greens burble away. And fried chicken. A barnyard of fried chicken. Yours for the asking.

Tell Denise what you would like and watch her spring into motion. With a quick pirouette she turns to snag a Styrofoam box and heads for the steamy kitchen, weaving higgledy-piggledy through a scrum of eight cooks, bound for

a pot of greens simmering on the back of the stove. A quick detour for a heaping scoop of mashed potatoes is followed by a swift dip into the closest kettle for what seems like a bushel of snap beans. Four or five pieces of fried chicken go on top of that. A sheet of waxed paper and brace of three biscuits on top of that. Total elapsed time: 45 seconds. Total calories: You can't count that high. —*J. T. E.*

GO AROUND TO THE BACK DOOR TO SEE THE KITCHEN CREW PREPARING PRODUCE. MRS. DEMPSEY STRIPS MOUNTAINS OF COLLARDS LEAF BY LEAF BEFORE THEY HIT THE KETTLES.

Vegetables

SNAP BEANS OR BUTTER BEANS

Snap beans and butter beans are Southern favorites, and no week would be complete at Mrs. Wilkes' without generous helpings of one or both.

Ham hock or pieces of ham
I 1/2 pounds green beans
I teaspoon salt
Pepper

Cook the ham in a small amount of boiling water for 10 to 15 minutes while you prepare the green beans. Trim the stems from the beans, wash, and snap to the desired length. Add the beans to the pot, making sure there is at least 1 inch of water. Season with salt and pepper to taste. Cook, covered, for 15 to 20 minutes, or until crisp but tender. Serves 6.
NOTE: Cook butter beans the same way as snap beans, but there may be some variation in cooking time.

PICKLED BEETS

If you peek at Mrs. Wilkes' own plate you will see a serving of pickled beets every day. "It makes everything good," she tells customers.

2 cups sugar
I cup white vinegar
3 tablespoons pickling spice
4 bay leaves
4 cups fresh cooked or I (32-ounce can) beets

Combine the sugar, vinegar, pickling spice, and bay leaves in a sauté pan and heat to a boil. Add the beets and simmer for about 5 minutes. These beets are good served hot or cold. They will keep in the refrigerator for several weeks. Yields about 4 cups.

BUTTER BEANS

DAUGHTER MARGIE MARTIN AND MRS. WILKES. IT WAS MARGIE'S IDEA TO COLLECT HER MOTHER'S RECIPES.

TUESDAY'S
BLACKBOARD
MENU

Fried Chicken

Baked Chicken and
Dressing

Roast Pork and
Dressing

Beef Stew

Sausage

Baked Ham

Collard Greens

Snap Beans

Okra and Tomatoes

Rice and Gravy

Mashed Potatoes

Candied Yams

Pickled Beets

FRIED CABBAGE

1 medium head cabbage
1/4 cup bacon drippings
Salt and pepper
3 tablespoons dairy sour cream

Wash, core, and cut the cabbage into 1/4-inch squares. Sauté the cabbage in the bacon drippings, stirring constantly, for about 1 minute, until tender and crisp but not wilted or cooked through. Season with salt and pepper to taste, then stir in the sour cream. Serves 4.

FRIED EGGPLANT

"People often tell us that good fried eggplant has a passing resemblance in flavor to fried oysters," says Margie.

1 medium eggplant
Salt and pepper
1/3 cup flour
2 eggs, beaten
1/3 cup cracker crumbs
Bacon drippings or salad oil

Pare and cut the eggplant crosswise into 1/4-inch slices. Sprinkle with salt, pepper, and flour. Dip into the egg, then into the cracker crumbs. Fry the eggplant in bacon drippings for about 6 to 8 minutes, until golden brown on both sides. Serve with catsup or chile sauce. Serves 4.

SCALLOPED EGGPLANT

1 medium eggplant, peeled and cubed
1/2 cup minced onion
2 teaspoons salt, plus more to taste
1 1/2 cups crumbled soda crackers
Pepper
1 cup milk
2 tablespoons melted butter

Preheat the oven to 375°. Bring a small amount of water to a boil and add the eggplant, onions, and 2 teaspoons salt. Boil for about 5 minutes, until the eggplant is tender but not mushy. Drain. Spread 3/4 cup of the crackers in a greased baking dish and layer with the eggplant and onions. Season with salt and pepper to taste. Sprinkle the remaining 3/4 cup crackers on top. Pour enough milk into the corners of the baking dish to cover the bottom. Pour the butter on top. Bake, uncovered, for 45 minutes. Serves about 4.

Fried Potatoes

1/4 cup bacon drippings or salad oil
1 cup sliced onions
4 cups pared and sliced potatoes
1 1/4 teaspoons salt
1/8 teaspoon pepper
Snipped parsley

Heat the bacon drippings in a skillet. Arrange the onions and potatoes in the skillet. Season with the salt and pepper. Simmer, covered, over low heat for 15 minutes. Uncover, turn the heat up slightly, and cook for 10 minutes more, or until the potatoes are golden brown and crispy on the bottom. Do not stir. Sprinkle with parsley, then fold in half like an omelet. Serves 4.

Zesty Carrots

6 carrots, pared and sliced
1/2 cup mayonnaise
1 tablespoon horseradish
1/2 teaspoon pepper
1/2 cup buttered bread crumbs

Preheat the oven to 300°. Bring a small amount of water to a boil and add the carrots. Boil until tender and drain. Combine the mayonnaise, horseradish, and pepper in a 1-quart casserole. Toss the mixture with the carrots, and sprinkle the bread crumbs on top. Bake for 20 minutes, or until lightly brown on top. Serves 6 to 8.

Macaroni and Cheese

A house favorite, this dish always prompts Mrs. Wilkes to contend that it's the cheese that's the main ingredient.

2 cups elbow macaroni
1/2 cup butter or margarine, melted
4 eggs, beaten to a froth
3 cups milk
2 cups grated sharp Cheddar cheese
Pinch of salt

Preheat the oven to 350°. Cook the macaroni in salted boiling water as directed on the package and drain. Return to the pot and add the butter, then the eggs and milk. Stir in the cheese and add salt to taste. Place in a greased 1 1/2-quart casserole and bake for about 30 minutes, or until the liquid is firm but not dry. Serves 4 to 6.

Succotash

A great way to get even the most recalcitrant child to eat his vegetables.

1 1/2 cups hot cooked or canned whole-kernel corn
1 1/2 cups hot cooked or canned green beans, lima beans, or shell beans
2 tablespoons butter or margarine
1/2 cup light cream
Salt and pepper

Combine the corn, beans, butter, and cream, and season with salt and pepper to taste. Heat. Serves 6.

Corn Pudding

2 tablespoons sugar
2 tablespoons flour
1/2 teaspoons salt
2 cups fresh or frozen whole-kernel corn, cooked and drained
2 eggs, well beaten
1 cup milk
1 tablespoon melted butter

Preheat the oven to 350°. Combine the sugar, flour, and salt. Stir into the corn and add the eggs and milk. Pour the butter into a 1 1/2-quart casserole, add the corn mixture, and mix. Bake for 45 minutes to 1 hour, until a toothpick inserted comes out clean. Serves 6 to 8.

CHEESE GRITS

Mrs. Wilkes' cheese grits can convert even a steadfast Yankee into a believer in this Southern staple.

1 cup regular grits (do not use quick-cooking grits)
4 cups water
1/4 cup butter
1 (6-ounce) package garlic cheese or sharp Cheddar cheese
1 teaspoon salt
2 egg yolks, beaten well
2 egg whites, beaten stiff
Cracker or dry bread crumbs

Preheat the ovent to 350°. Cook the grits in the water according to the package's directions. Slowly add the butter, cheese, and salt. Add the egg yolks and fold in the egg whites. Pour into a greased 1 1/2-quart casserole. Sprinkle cracker crumbs on top. Bake for 45 minutes. Serves 6 to 8.

TOMATO AND OKRA GUMBO

"People are always asking me how to make this," says Mrs. Wilkes. "It's a good accompaniment to most anything on your plate."

8 medium tomatoes, chopped, or 1 (28-ounce)
  can tomatoes
2 pounds fresh or frozen baby okra, cut into
  1/2-inch pieces
1/2 teaspoon salt
1 tablespoon butter or margarine
3 strips bacon, fried to a crisp and crumbled

Combine the tomatoes, okra, salt, and butter in a saucepan. Cook, covered, over medium heat for 20 minutes, or until tender. Sprinkle the bacon on top. Serves 8.

CORN BREAD DRESSING

"Our friends tell us that their child won't eat their corn bread dressing after tasting Mrs. Wilkes'," says Margie. "We use so much stock, you don't need gravy."

4 cups crumbled corn bread
2 cups crumbled toast crumbs
4 1/2 cups hot chicken, pork, or turkey stock
3 hard-boiled eggs, chopped
1 cup grated celery
1/2 cup grated onion
1/2 cup grated bell pepper
Salt and pepper (optional)

Preheat the oven to 375°. Combine the corn bread and the toast crumbs and add the stock. Cover and allow to sit for 5 or 10 minutes. Add the eggs, celery, onion, and bell pepper. Bake in well-greased pan for 30 to 40 minutes. Since the stock and bread are already seasoned, add salt and pepper only if desired. Yields 8 cups.

STEAMED CABBAGE

The fragrance of this Monday menu workhorse can be detected above that of the flowering nasturtiums on West Jones Street.

3 strips salt pork or bacon, cut into small pieces
2 medium heads cabbage, cut, washed, and drained
1/2 cup pork or bacon drippings
Salt

Sauté the pork until brown. Put the cabbage in a saucepan. Add the drippings and browned meat. Cover and bring to a boil over medium heat. Stir and let steam for 5 minutes. Add salt to taste. Serves 8 to 10.

Sema Says

"Do not make the mistake of cooking meat or vegetables on high heat. This takes away the flavor and food value."

Mixed Vegetable Casserole

6 tablespoons butter or margarine
1 cup chopped onion
1 cup chopped celery
4 cups fresh chopped vegetables (carrots, peas, and corn),
    or 1 (32-ounce) bag frozen mixed vegetables, cooked
    and drained
1 (7-ounce) can water chestnuts, drained
1 (11 1/2-ounce) can cream of chicken soup
1 cup mayonnaise
1 cup cracker crumbs

Preheat the oven to 350°. Melt 4 tablespoons of the butter and sauté the onions and celery until tender. Add the vegetables, water chestnuts, soup, and mayonnaise; and mix well. Pour into a lightly greased 9 by 13 by 2-inch casserole. Melt the remaining 2 tablespoons butter in a small skillet, stir in the cracker crumbs, and sprinkle over the casserole. Bake for 30 minutes, until brown on top and bubbly. Serves 8.

Spicy Black-Eyed Peas

Black-eyed peas are a traditional good luck dish on New Year's Day. This spicy rendition of a regional favorite brings good luck throughout the year!

1 (16-ounce) bag dry black-eyed peas
1 cup chopped onion
1 cup uncooked rice
1 pound sausage, browned
1/2 green pepper, chopped
1/4 teaspoon Tabasco sauce (optional)
Salt and pepper

Cook the peas according to package's directions, until almost done. Add the remaining ingredients and simmer until the peas are tender. Serves 8 to 12.
NOTE: If the peas or rice appear to be dry, add additional water.

FRIED OKRA

Use the smallest, most delicate okra pods you can find.

1 1/2 pounds fresh okra
Salt and pepper
Flour
Corn oil, or other cooking oil

Cut the okra crosswise (not too thin) into 3/4-inch slices.
Season with salt and pepper. Toss the okra in flour and shake
off the excess. Heat about 1/2 inch of oil in a skillet. Fry the okra
over medium heat. Stir and turn until light brown and tender.
Remove with a spatula and drain on paper towels. Serves 4.

POTATOES IN CREAM SAUCE

2 tablespoons butter or margarine
2 tablespoons flour
2 cups milk
4 cups cooked small new potatoes
Salt and pepper
Grated mild white or yellow cheese (optional)

To make the sauce, melt the butter in a small saucepan. Add the
flour and stir until well blended. Add the milk and cook until
bubbly and thickened. In a large saucepan, combine the sauce
and potatoes. Cook slowly until the sauce thickens and the
potatoes are hot. Season with salt and pepper to taste and add
the cheese. Serves 4 to 6.

Skillet Squash au Gratin

Grated cheese and onion add interest to this summer vegetable.

1/4 cup butter or margarine
4 cups thinly sliced yellow squash
1 sliced onion
1 teaspoon salt
Pinch of pepper
1/4 cup cold water
1/2 cup grated cheese

Melt the butter in a saucepan. Add the squash, onion, salt, pepper, and water. Cook, covered, for 10 to 15 minutes, or until the squash is tender. Sprinkle the cheese on top. Serves 4.

Puffy Mallow Sweet Potatoes

4 or 5 medium sweet potatoes, pared
1 cup pineapple or orange juice
1/4 cup butter or margarine
1 egg, slightly beaten
1 teaspoon salt
1/4 teaspoon cinnamon
8 marshmallows

Cut the sweet potatoes into large chunks. Cook, uncovered, in pineapple juice for about 20 minutes, or until tender. Drain, reserving the juice. Preheat the oven to 350°. Mash the potatoes well. Add the butter, egg, salt, cinnamon, and about 1/3 cup of the reserved juice. Beat with a spoon or electric mixer until creamy. Spoon into an 8-inch round baking dish. Lightly press the marshmallows into the top. Bake, uncovered, for 30 minutes, or until marshmallows are golden brown. Serves 6.

Savannah Red Rice

The Low Country's penchant for red rice is reflected in the fact that this dish has remained on the menu throughout the decades.

2 medium onions, diced
2 medium bell peppers, diced
Bacon drippings
2 cups cooked rice
6 to 8 tomatoes, chopped and cooked, or 1 (16-ounce) can tomatoes
1 cup tomato sauce or catsup
1/2 teaspoon Tabasco sauce
4 strips bacon, fried to a crisp and crumbled
Salt and pepper
2 tablespoons grated Parmesan cheese

Preheat the oven to 325°. Brown the onions and bell peppers in bacon drippings. In a large mixing bowl, combine the rice, onions and peppers, tomatoes, tomato sauce, Tabasco, and bacon. Season with salt and pepper to taste. Mix well. Pour into a greased casserole, sprinkle the cheese on to. Bake for 30 minutes, or until rice is dry enough to separate. Serves 4 to 6.
NOTE: You may want to add 1 pound of cooked shrimp, sausage, pork, or ham.

Squash Casserole

"I've been making this recipe for as long as I can remember," says Mrs. Wilkes. "The secret is the cornflakes," she adds with a wink. "They keep it together."

4 pounds yellow squash, sliced
1 medium onion, diced
1 teaspoon pepper
1 teaspoon salt
2 cups cornflakes, crushed
1/4 cup butter or margarine, melted
1 (10-1/2 ounce) can cream of mushroom soup
1 cup grated American cheese

Preheat the oven to 350°. Combine the squash and onion in a saucepan. Pour in some salted water and cook over medium heat for about 20 minutes. Drain and mash. Add the pepper, salt, cornflakes, margarine, and soup and mix. Place in a baking dish and cover with the cheese. Bake for 20 minutes. Serves 8.

Baked Cauliflower

1 head cauliflower
2 tablespoons butter or margarine
2 tablespoons flour
Pinch of pepper
1/2 teaspoon salt
1 cup milk
1 cup grated Cheddar cheese (optional)

Be sure to use a crisp, white cauliflower head, as free from spots as possible. Remove the outer leaves and stalks. Wash and core as much as possible without altering the shape. Bring a small amount of water, salted to taste, to a boil. Add the cauliflower and boil, covered, for 20 to 30 minutes. Drain the cauliflower and place in a greased casserole. Preheat the oven to 350°. Melt the butter in a small saucepan. Add the flour, pepper, and salt and stir until bubbly and well blended. Add the milk and cheese and continue cooking until bubbly and thickened. Pour the sauce over the cauliflower and bake for 15 to 20 minutes, or until the sauce is bubbly. Serves 4.

FRIED CAULIFLOWER

1 medium head cauliflower, separated into florets
1 egg
1/4 cup milk
Salt and pepper
2 cups cracker meal
Vegetable oil or fat

Bring some salted water to a boil, add the cauliflower, and boil for 10 minutes, or until tender. Drain and let cool. Combine the egg and milk, add salt and pepper to taste, and beat slightly. Dip floret into the egg mixture, roll in cracker meal, and drop in deep, hot oil. Cook until brown. Serves 4.

GLAZED CARROTS

1 (16-ounce) bag whole baby carrots
1 cup granulated sugar
1/2 cup butter or margarine

Cook the carrots for about 20 to 40 minutes, until almost tender. Drain well, then pat dry with paper towels. Roll the carrots in the granulated sugar. Melt the butter in a saucepan, add the carrots, and simmer, turning often, until glazed. Serves 4 to 6.

Sweet Potato Soufflé

Coconut, lemon rind, and raisins are a bright surprise. "A lot of people buy my cookbook just to get this recipe," says Mrs. Wilkes.

4 pounds sweet potatoes, pared and sliced
1 1/2 cups sugar
2 eggs
1/2 cup raisins
Grated rind and juice of 1 lemon
1/2 teaspoon cinnamon
1/2 teaspoon nutmeg
1/2 cup evaporated milk
1/2 cup chopped pecans
1/2 cup butter or margarine, melted
1/2 cup shredded coconut
Miniature marshmallows

Place the potatoes in a pot and add enough salted water to cover. Cook until tender. Drain. Preheat the oven to 350°. Mash and whip the potatoes. Add the remaining ingredients (except marshmallows) and mix well. Pour into a greased casserole dish. Bake for 30 minutes. Remove from the oven and cover with marshmallows. Return to the oven and continue cooking until brown. Serves 8.

Corn on the Cob

"We use the prettiest, freshest yellow corn we can find," declares Marcia. "Bicolor corn is best on the cob," adds Ronnie.

6 ears tender corn, shucked and broken in half
1/2 cup sugar
2 tablespoons butter
Salt and pepper (optional)

Combine the corn, sugar, and butter in a saucepan. Add enough water to cover the corn. Cover and heat to a boil. Boil for 5 minutes. Remove from the heat and serve. If desired, add more butter, salt, and pepper. Serves 6.

Sema Says

Of the size of her kitchen, Mrs. Wilkes says, "I always tell my girls they don't have to run for anything here. Everything's close at hand."

MASHED POTATOES

Every day Mrs. Wilkes' orders 100 pounds each of sweet and white potatoes. "But if I know that the Girl Scouts are in town," says Ronnie, "I order more!"

9 medium potatoes, peeled and sliced thinly
6 tablespoons butter or margarine
3/4 cup hot milk
Salt and pepper

Add the potatoes to water and boil until tender. Drain. With a potato masher or electric mixer, mash the potatoes thoroughly, until no lumps remain. Melt the butter in a small saucepan; add the milk, and heat until hot (do not boil). With a masher, gradually add the butter and milk to make the potatoes fluffy and creamy. Season with salt and pepper to taste. Serves 8 to 10.

CREAM-STYLE CORN

"The best corn I've ever had is grown by my cousin in Ellabelle, Georgia," asserts Marcia. "But my second granny, Inez Smith, of Arden, Georgia, made this cream-style corn. It was good enough for me to sneak out of the refrigerator at night!"

1 dozen medium ears sweet corn
1/2 cup butter, margarine, or bacon drippings
3/4 tablespoon salt
1 teaspoon pepper
2 tablespoons sugar
2 tablespoons flour
1 cup milk

Cut the kernels off the corn cobs and scrape the cobs to get the juices. Discard the cobs. Cook the corn with its juices, butter, salt, pepper, and sugar in a heavy saucepan over low heat for 15 minutes, frequently stirring with a wooden ladle to make sure the corn does not stick. Add the flour to the milk and stir to thicken. Add to the corn. Let simmer for a few minutes and remove from the heat. If it's not thick enough, simmer longer. If it's too thick, add additional milk or water. Serves 6 to 8.

BLACK-EYED PEAS

1 cup dried black-eyed peas, picked over and washed
6 cups hot water
1 slice salt pork
2 tablespoons minced onion
1 teaspoon salt

Place the peas in a kettle with the water, salt pork, onion, and salt. Cover and bring to a boil. Reduce the heat and simmer for 2 1/2 hours, or until tender. Drain. Serves 4.

Stewed Tomatoes

A sweet reminder that the tomato is indeed a fruit. Stewed tomatoes increase in natural flavor when seasoned with brown sugar.

2 teaspoons brown sugar
4 teaspoons flour
1 (28-ounce) can tomatoes, or 2 1/2 cups quartered
   and peeled fresh tomatoes
1 teaspoon salt
4 teaspoons butter, margarine, or bacon drippings
Pepper
1 teaspoon minced onion (optional)

Combine the sugar and flour and add remaining ingredients. Simmer for 10 minutes. Serves 4.

Rutabaga

These are sometimes called yellow turnips. They are best in the fall.

4 pounds rutabagas, peeled and sliced
2 tablespoons sugar
1 tablespoon salt
Pepper
1/2 cup butter or margarine, or 4 tablespoons bacon
   drippings

Place the rutabagas in a saucepan. Cover with water. Add the sugar, salt, and pepper. Cover and cook over medium heat for about 1 hour; drain. Add the butter, mash, and serve hot. Serves 8.

Candied Yams

4 pounds (about 6 medium-sized) yams, pared
1 1/2 cups sugar
1 lemon
1/2 cup butter or margarine

Slice the potatoes thickly and place in a large saucepan. Cover with boiling water and salt lightly. Cook, covered, until almost tender. Pour out almost all of the water, leaving 1/2 inch water in the bottom of the saucepan. Add the sugar, lemon, and butter and cook over medium heat for 30 to 45 minutes, or until the juice is slightly thickened. Serves 8 to 10.

SUE'S POTATOES AU GRATIN

This is a signature dish hereabouts. It is just a bit tangy—the unmistakable stamp of long-time cook Susie Mae Kennell, who developed it.

6 cups potatoes, peeled and sliced thinly
1 cup mayonnaise
2 tablespoons prepared mustard
2 tablespoons white vinegar
1 medium onion, grated
1/2 cup grated Cheddar cheese

Add the potatoes to the water and boil until tender. Drain. Preheat the oven to 350°. With a potato masher or electric mixer, mash the potatoes thoroughly, until no lumps remain. Add the mayonnaise, mustard, vinegar, and onion. Place in a casserole and top with the cheese. Bake for about 15 minutes, or until the mixture bubbles and the cheese is melted. Serves 6 to 8.

HOPPIN' JOHN

Sprinkled with hot pepper and vinegar, this is Ronnie's all-time favorite. It's served at Mrs. Wilkes' on New Year's Day.

2 cups dried black-eyed peas or red field peas
4 cups water
1/2 cup chopped onion (optional)
1 ham hock, or 1/4 pound pork or hog jowl
2 cups cooked rice
2 tablespoons butter or margarine

Place the peas, water, onion, and ham in a pot. Boil over low heat until tender. Add the rice and butter and cook slowly until ready to serve. Serves 10 to 12.
NOTE: The rice can be cooked in the peas. Follow the directions for the peas, and put the rice in the peas about 30 minutes before the peas are done. The flavor is better!

Some etymologists believe that Hoppin' John—a dish composed of black-eyed peas and rice and sundry seasonings—is a corruption of the Caribbean term *pois à pigeon*, which, with a relaxing of the tongue may well have become *pwa-pee-jon*, and, over time, Hoppin' John.

—*J. T. E.*

We Southerners love fresh greens—collard, creecy, kale, beet, mustard, turnip, rape, poke, dock, and lamb's quarters being just a few of our favorites. The most common of the seemingly infinite varieties are collard greens and turnip greens. Collard greens are a type of kale and are arguably best after the first frost of the fall. Turnip greens are the true leaves of a bulbous root. As for the difference in taste, some consider the collard to taste earthier, the turnip more astringent.

—J. T. E.

OLD-FASHIONED CREAMED ASPARAGUS

2 pounds fresh or 2 (10-ounce) packages frozen asparagus
1 cup water
3 tablespoons butter or margarine
4 1/2 teaspoons flour
1 small (5-ounce) can evaporated milk
1/2 teaspoon salt
1/8 teaspoon pepper

Prepare and boil the asparagus for 10 to 15 minutes; drain, reserving the broth. Leave the stalks whole or cut into 1-inch lengths as desired. Melt the butter in a saucepan and stir in the flour. Add the milk, salt, pepper, and asparagus broth; cook until bubbly and thickened. Add additional water if the sauce is too thick. Pour the mixture over the asparagus. Heat just to a boil (avoid mashing the asparagus) and stir gently. Serves 6 to 8.

WHITE RICE

"So many cooks don't know how to prepare rice the right way," asserts Mrs. Wilkes. "They have trouble getting the texture they want." Here's her fail-safe method for great rice every time.

1 cup uncooked rice
2 cups water
1 teaspoon salt
1 teaspoon vegetable oil
1/2 teaspoon white vinegar

Combine all of the ingredients in a medium saucepan; heat to a boil. Boil until almost all of the water has been absorbed by the rice. Reduce the heat to a simmer. Cover and continue cooking over low heat for about 15 to 20 minutes, until the rice is tender. Serves 4 to 6.

Brown Rice

3 strips bacon
1/2 cup chopped green onions, including tops
1 cup diced celery
1 cup sliced mushrooms
3 cups cooked rice
2 tablespoons soy sauce
1 egg, slightly beaten

Fry the bacon in a large skillet. Remove from the skillet, drain on paper towels, and crumble. Place the onions and celery in the bacon drippings and sauté until tender. Add the mushrooms, rice, and soy sauce. Cook for 10 minutes over low heat, stirring occasionally. Stir in the beaten egg and cook until the egg is done. Add the bacon and mix well. Extra soy sauce may be added. Serve with rice. Serves 6.

Turnip Greens

How do you spot a Yankee at Mrs. Wilkes'? He motions toward the turnip greens and says, "Please pass the spinach."

1 bunch fresh turnip greens with roots
1 medium piece salt pork
1 cup water
1 teaspoon salt
2 tablespoons bacon drippings, butter, or margarine
Pinch of sugar (optional)

Strip the stems from the greens (unless they're very tender) and wash thoroughly. Place in a saucepan and add the pork, water, and salt. Cook, covered, for 45 minutes over medium heat, or until tender. Remove the pork and pour the greens into a colander to drain. Place in a pan and chop scissor-like with two knives. If necessary, add more salt to taste. Keep hot and add the bacon drippings and a pinch of sugar. Serves 4 to 6.
NOTE: Except for the roots, cook collard greens and mustard greens the same way.

COLLARD GREENS

Every year the two brothers who own Promised Land Farm, near Savannnah, host a collard green festival. The public is invited to pull their own greens. Watch for the signs at Mrs. Wilkes', telling of the upcoming event.

Follow the recipe for Turnip Greens (page 127).

CREOLE EGGPLANT

Remember to salt the eggplant after it has been peeled and cubed and allow it to drain on a paper towel for 20 minutes before proceeding with the recipe. And don't forget the cornflakes!

3 medium eggplants, peeled and cubed
4 tablespoons bacon drippings
1 teaspoon salt
1/2 cup minced bell pepper
1/2 cup minced onion
6 tomatoes, chopped and cooked, or 1 (28-ounce) can
     tomatoes and juice
1/2 cup catsup
1 cup cornflakes
Grated Parmesan cheese

Cook the eggplant with 2 tablespoons of the bacon drippings and salt for about 5 minutes. This should yield about 1 quart of cooked eggplant. Preheat the oven to 325°. Brown the bell pepper and onion in the remaining 2 tablespoons bacon drippings. Combine the eggplant, bell pepper and onions, tomatoes, catsup, and cornflakes. Mix and pour into a baking dish. Sprinkle cheese on top and bake for 30 minutes. Serves about 8.
NOTE: Very good reheated.

COLLARD GREENS

Barbecue Corn

In the 1950s, Mrs. Wilkes began serving this original recipe, and it quickly became a favorite of the boarders.

1 pound ground chuck
1 medium bell pepper, chopped
1/2 cup chopped celery
1 medium onion, chopped
1 teaspoon salt
1 cup catsup
1 teaspoon chile powder
1/2 teaspoon garlic powder
1 (16-ounce) can whole kernel corn, drained
Pinch of pepper
Dash of Tabasco sauce (optional)

Brown the ground beef in a large skillet. Drain and return to the skillet. Add the pepper, celery, and onion and stir until browned. Add the remaining ingredients and mix well. Heat until hot, then reduce heat and simmer for 15 minutes. Add more salt and pepper to taste. Serves 4.

English Peas and Noodles

A favorite Friday feature, this peas and noodles combination rates as Southern comfort food.

1 (10-ounce) package frozen or 1 1/4 cups fresh tiny
   English peas
1 small onion, minced (optional)
1 tablespoon bacon drippings or ham
1/4 cup finely chopped mushrooms
1/2 cup dumpling-type noodles
1/2 cup Cream Sauce (page 42)

Cook the peas and onion in the bacon drippings. Add the mushrooms and noodles. When the noodles are done, make the sauce, and add. Simmer to a near boil. Serves 6 to 8.

 **Breads**

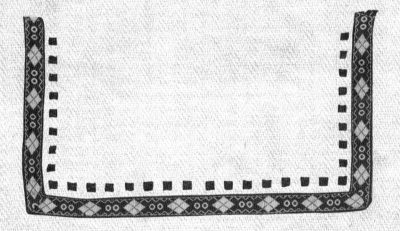

Three Generations of Strong Women

Mrs. Wilkes' Boardinghouse came of age in a day when the men took their seats at the dining room table before the women, despite the fact that women—nearly always women—were the ones charged with the labors of baking and broiling, stewing and frying the food that graced the family table. The rationale was that the men needed to eat the lion's share, the choicest cuts of meat, the great bounty of the Southern garden, so that they could return to the fields, refueled, refreshed, and ready to plow the back forty.

Women were thought to be the fairer sex, the weaker gender. A strapping man of Mrs. Wilkes' generation wouldn't stoop to engage in women's work, for his brawn and brain were required elsewhere. True, such roles are now consigned to memory. Viewed from a modern-day remove, this all might best be understood as a calculated deceit, perpetrated by Southern women in an effort to carve out a space all their own, a world where steel magnolias bloom.

Such duplicity wouldn't surprise Ronnie Thompson one whit. After working most of his adult life alongside a strong-willed female kitchen crew, he has come to regard Mrs. Wilkes and her ilk with unabashed awe. "Back when she was serving three meals a day, in the afternoon, just before supper, she would pull out four chairs from the table and make them into almost a little bed," he recalls. "Mrs. Wilkes would sleep for maybe twenty minutes like that, and then jump right back up for supper. And when she got home at night, she would stay up until two in the morning vacuuming. She doesn't know what idle time is, and she doesn't put up with foolishness."

Mrs. Wilkes had no intent of bequeathing her legacy of hard work to successive generations. Indeed, she did all she could to dissuade her daughter, Margie Martin, from following in her footsteps. But in 1986, after a twenty-year career with the local electric company, Margie found herself stepping in to help out when her father fell ill and Mrs. Wilkes needed another hand in the dining room. From that time forward, she has worked

as the restaurant's business manager and bookkeeper. Truth be told, though, she had been a strong influence in the business since back in 1974 when, spurred by numerous guest requests for the secret to her mother's eggy squash casserole and feathery, baking powder biscuits, she began compiling recipes for a cookbook.

In April 1987, Mrs. Wilkes was a featured cook at Lord & Taylor's *Focus America* festival in New York City.

"I never ever had too much time for cooking," recalls Margie. "I did so many other things. But so many people would say to us, 'I sure do wish I could learn to cook like this,' that I said, 'Well, I believe I will try it.' My husband told me, 'You just have to get somebody to do that for you; you can't do that yourself with all you have to do.' But I said to him, 'I can and I will.' From then on, when we went on vacation, I would take my note pad and I'd say to my mother, 'How do you do this, and how do you do that, and what do you do here, and what do you do there?'" In January of 1976, the first 3,000 spiral-bound copies of *Famous Recipes* rolled off the press. Over a quarter of a million copies have been sold in the past twenty-five years, winning Margie the last laugh and the ladies of Mrs. Wilkes' Boardinghouse a tidy sum. Indeed, the book you hold in your hands today owes its origins to the work of recipe gathering, testing, and tasting that Margie began so many years ago.

Despite the importance of the boardinghouse as a family business, it has always been a matter of more than mere enterprise for the Wilkes women. For Margie's daughter, Marcia, who spent her early years there under the watchful eye of the upstairs maid, Lessie Bates, after-

DRAG QUEEN LADY CHABLIS, MADE FAMOUS BY JOHN BERENDT'S *MIDNIGHT IN THE GARDEN OF GOOD AND EVIL*, ALSO ENJOYS THE DOWN-HOME FLAVOR OF A MEAL AT MRS. WILKES'.

school hours at the gray brick townhouse provided an entrée to the world of her ancestors. "My great-grandmother, Mr. Wilkes' mother, lived on the parlor floor above the restaurant when I was young," recalls Marcia. "As a little girl, I remember her as my best friend. I looked up to her so much and wanted her to go everywhere we went. There was a trip we all took to California in 1954. I remember saying that we could take the station wagon and make a bed in the back so that she could nap on the way. I wanted her to come so very badly. You know, the women in our family have been so blessed with long lives. To know your great-grandmother like I did, like my daughter Emily knows Mrs. Wilkes, well, that's something special. When I was working as a flight attendant for Delta, back before I started helping out here, I don't think I truly appreciated the importance of that time. Now I do."

For Marcia's daughter, Emily, now in her early twenties, the multigenerational bonds are even stronger, more immediate. "I grew up in the business," says Emily. "I can remember being really little and listening to stories from Mama, Mrs. Wilkes, about how she would get out in the yard back on the farm and wring chicken necks. I remember playing with the biscuit dough

FOUR GENERATIONS OF STRONG WOMEN, MARGIE MARTIN AND HER MOTHER, MRS. WILKES, AND EMILY THOMPSON AND HER MOTHER, MARCIA.

when I was tiny. I started out in the summers during high school, rolling silverware for her. She taught me to do everything perfect, to twist those rolls tight. But I've never gotten involved in the day-to-day business. My parents don't want me to go into the business. They know it's too hard, and I've seen how much Mama has worked. Plus I don't know if I could live up to her standards. But if somebody asks me, 'Hey, are you related to Mrs. Wilkes? Is that your family?' I just about blush with pride."   —J. T. E.

Breads

BOARDINGHOUSE-STYLE BISCUITS

Mrs. Wilkes' serves about 630 biscuits a day. The Wilkes family loves these with Georgia cane syrup, and eats them morning, noon, and night—even as dessert!

2 cups self-rising flour
1/2 teaspoon baking powder
1 teaspoon sugar
2 tablespoons shortening
2 tablespoons butter or margarine
1/3 cup buttermilk
1/3 cup whole milk
1 tablespoon plus 1 teaspoon water

Preheat the oven to 450°. Grease an 8 by 8 by 2-inch baking pan well. Sift the flour, baking powder, and sugar into a bowl. Cut in the shortening and butter until the mixture resembles coarse cornmeal. Make a well in the center of the flour and pour in the buttermilk and milk. Mix lightly and quickly with your hands to form a dough moist enough to leave the sides of the bowl. Turn onto a lightly floured surface. Knead by picking up the sides of the dough away from you while pressing down with the palms of your hands and pushing the dough away. Repeat 6 or 7 times. Work the dough into a large ball while kneading. Keep your fingers dry by frequently dipping them in dry flour. Pinch off portions of dough for desired size biscuit. Press lightly to make the biscuits look flat on the pan. Make sure the biscuits touch each other. Bake for 15 minutes. Yields about 8 boardinghouse-sized biscuits.

DINERS SOMETIMES
SUSPECT THAT THE BISCUITS
ARE FROZEN BECAUSE
THEY'RE SO PERFECT.
BUT, NO, THEY'RE PATTED
OUT BY HAND—MORE
THAN 600 EACH DAY.

WEDNESDAY'S
BLACKBOARD
MENU

———

Fried Chicken

Beef Stew

Meat Loaf

BBQ Pork

Baked Ham

Collard Greens

Snap Beans

Squash

Rice and Gravy

Macaroni and Cheese

Brown Rice

Potato Salad

Pickled Beets

Candied Yams

Okra and Tomatoes

AUNT MINNIE SHARP'S MIRACLE ROLLS

Aunt Minnie's husband had the post office in Austin, Georgia. Mrs. Wilkes remembers, "Her rolls were better than anyone else's. They were the best rolls in creation."

3 packages dry yeast
1/2 cup warm water
5 cups self-rising flour
1/4 cup sugar
1 teaspoon baking soda
1 cup shortening
2 cups lukewarm buttermilk

Preheat the oven to 350°. Dissolve the yeast in the warm water and set aside. Mix the flour, sugar, and baking soda. Cut in the shortening. Add the buttermilk and yeast. Mix well. Place half of the dough on a floured cloth, pat out, and cut with a biscuit cutter. Repeat with the remaining dough. Let the dough rise to double thickness before baking. Bake for 10 to 15 minutes. Yields about 2 dozen.

CRANBERRY MUFFINS

Use leftover Thanksgiving cranberries to make these muffins.

1 cup chopped fresh cranberries
3/4 cup sugar
2 cups flour
1/2 teaspoon baking soda
3/4 teaspoon salt
1 egg, beaten
3/4 cup sour milk
1/4 cup melted shortening

Preheat the oven to 400°. Combine the cranberries and 1/2 cup of the sugar. Sift together the flour, baking soda, salt, and the remaining 1/4 cup sugar. Mix the egg, milk, and shortening. Make a well in the dry ingredients and add the liquid all at once. Stir until blended. Add the cranberries, mixing slightly. Fill the cups of a greased muffin pan 2/3 full. Bake for 20 minutes. Yields about 1 dozen.

Pumpkin Bread

"Canned pumpkin is actually better and more reliable than fresh pumpkin," claims Mrs. Wilkes. Nuts and raisins add sweetness and crunch.

2/3 cup shortening
2 2/3 cups sugar
4 eggs
1 (15-ounce) can pumpkin
2/3 cup water
3 1/3 cups self-rising flour
1 teaspoon ground cinnamon
1 teaspoon ground cloves
2/3 cup nuts
2/3 cup raisins

Preheat the oven to 350°. In a large bowl, cream the shortening and sugar until light and fluffy. Add the eggs, pumpkin, and water. Add 3 cups of the flour, cinnamon, and cloves, beating after each addition. Mix the remaining 1/3 cup flour, nuts, and raisins in a small bowl. Add to the batter and mix until well blended. Pour into 2 greased 9 by 5 by 3-inch loaf pans. Bake for 1 hour. Yields 2 loaves.

Spoon Bread

Sweet corn bread so soft and moist that it has to be served with a spoon.

3 cups of self-rising yellow cornmeal
2 eggs
2 cups buttermilk
Pinch of baking soda
1/2 teaspoon salt
3 tablespoons melted butter

Preheat the oven to in 350°. Mix the cornmeal, eggs, buttermilk, soda, and salt. Add the butter and pour into a greased baking dish. The batter should be very smooth before baking; add more milk if needed. Bake for 25 to 30 minutes. Serve with your dinner while still hot. Serves 8 to 10.

Hush Puppies

The story behind hush puppies is an old one: Southern cooks would throw these to the hungry whining dogs (who were driven crazy by the delicious smells of cooking food) to keep them quiet. Hence, "Hush, puppies!"

2 cups cornmeal
1 cup self-rising flour
1 tablespoon baking powder
1 teaspoon salt
1 teaspoon pepper
2 tablespoons grated onion
2 eggs
1 tablespoon catsup
1 small (5-ounce) can evaporated milk
Cooking oil

Sift the cornmeal and flour together. Add the baking powder, salt, pepper, and onion. Beat in the eggs and catsup. Add the evaporated milk and enough water to make a stiff batter. Using a teaspoon, drop the batter into hot oil, dipping the spoon in water before returning it to the batter each time. Fry and turn each hush puppy until golden brown on both sides. Yields about 2 dozen.

Sour Cream Baby Biscuits

A spoonful of peach preserves with these little biscuits and a hot cup of tea will make your ladies' luncheon a great hit!

1 cup dairy sour cream
2 cups self-rising flour
1 cup butter or margarine, melted

Preheat the oven to 400°. Blend the sour cream into the flour. Add the butter and stir until well blended. Drop the mixture by heaping teaspoonfuls into the cups of a miniature muffin tin to fill 2/3 full. Bake for 15 minutes, or until puffed and golden. Yields about 4 dozen.
NOTE: These biscuits can be frozen. Reheat at 325° until warm.

CORN BREAD MUFFINS

The effervescent Florrie Simpson Leach, Mrs. Wilkes' longest
serving cook, claims these as her specialty.

I 1/4 cups cornmeal
3/4 cup all-purpose flour, sifted
I teaspoon salt
I teaspoon baking powder
2/3 cup milk
1/3 cup salad oil
I egg

Preheat the oven to 425°. Mix the dry and liquid ingredients
separately. Pour the liquid into the dry mixture. Stir with a
spoon until well mixed. Fill the cups of a greased 12-cup muffin
tin about 2/3 full. Bake for 25 minutes. Yields about 1 dozen.
NOTE: For corn bread squares, bake in an 8 by 8 by 2-inch
pan. For cracklin' bread, add I cup pork cracklings.

Erin's Breakfast Roll-ups

Ronnie's nephew's wife, Erin Thompson, created this new dish. These roll-ups are as pretty as they are satisfying.

2 cans crescent rolls
6 eggs, scrambled
6 strips bacon, fried to a crisp and crumbled, or
   1 cupcooked and crumbled sausage
1 1/2 cups grated sharp Cheddar cheese
1 small tomato, diced
1 small onion, chopped
1 medium green pepper, chopped

Preheat the oven to 375°. Separate 1 can of rolls and place them on a large baking sheet in a circular sun pattern, with the points on the long sides touching each other and the third points touching the outside edge of the pan. Separate the remaining can of rolls and place them slightly overlapping the first layer in the same direction to make extra room for the filling. Layer the eggs, bacon, cheese, tomato, onion, and green pepper on top of the dough all around the circle. Take the outstretched points (the sun's rays) and cover the stuffing. Tuck the points under to seal. Bake for 15 minutes, or until golden brown. Carefully loosen the baked circle and slide onto a large serving platter. Serves 8.
NOTE: Decorate the center of the ring with a steaming bowl of buttered grits. Garnish with fresh sliced fruit.

Fried Corn Bread Rounds

These are a Mrs. Wilkes original, dating back to the farm days. Great with buttermilk!

1/2 cup water
1 tablespoon bacon drippings
1/2 cup self-rising cornmeal
1/8 teaspoon salt
Butter

Stir the water and bacon drippings into the cornmeal and salt. Pour half of the mixture onto a well-greased hot griddle. Cook until brown, turn, and brown on the other side. Repeat. Spread with butter while still hot. Serves 2.

 Desserts

Mrs. Wilkes' Today

Sometime in the early 1980s, after what seemed liked an interminable affair with all manner of so-called continental cuisines, we Americans finally came around to embracing our native dishes, our regional specialties like baked beans from Boston, steamed stone crabs from Miami, and the filé-gilded gumbos of New Orleans, not to mention fry bread from Arizona, smoked salmon from Washington state, and, yes, the foods of Low Country Georgia like red rice, hoppin' John, and stewed tomatoes studded with okra. Not surprisingly, more than a few of these new disciples of American cookery beat a path to Mrs. Wilkes' door.

It was along about this time—say 1987 or so—that Mrs. Wilkes finally agreed to post a discreet sign by the curb in front of her dining room. For the longest time, if you asked her why she didn't hang out a shingle to announce her presence, Mrs. Wilkes would fix you with a sweet smile and say, "Why, that wouldn't do, that wouldn't look at all like home." But as the crowds grew, the family realized that something had to be done. "Our neighbors were getting tired of strangers ringing their doorbell, looking to be fed," says Ronnie Thompson. "More and more people came and it began to happen with regularity. And then there were the Girl Scouts. It seems like they always got lost, walking over from their headquarters at the Lowe House."

Though the restaurant had long enjoyed the status of national media darling, winning praise in every publication from *Business Week* to *Bon Appetit*, by the late 1980s the queries were coming from overseas. "Somebody phoned to ask if I would come cook in a castle in Belgium," recalls Mrs. Wilkes. "I told them if they let me take my daughter and granddaughter, I'd consider doing it." On November 20, 1986, the three women made the trip, loading down their suitcases with a sack of soft winter wheat flour for biscuits, a mess of turnip greens, and a bushel of okra, to name just a few of the Southern staples they imported to the land of *moules et frites*. The meal, staged in the Kasteel Belvedere not far from Brussels, was a rousing success.

Next came a sojourn in Japan, sponsored in part by the Georgia Department of Industry and Trade. For a January 1989 promotion entitled *Georgia on My Mind: American Homestyle Cooking*, the entire Wilkes clan boarded a jumbo jet bound for Tokyo and the New Otami Hotel. The

Japanese were ready, primed to taste some of the South's fabled cookery. To prepare for the event, the hotel had even sent its assistant grand chef Yoshinao Nagumo to study with Mrs. Wilkes in Savannah. "He had a hard time with pinches and dashes," recalls Mrs. Wilkes. "He wanted everything to be a science." And what did Mrs. Wilkes think of the Japanese interpretations of her down-home dishes? "Well, it was pretty good," she said at the time, "but they put squid on the spaghetti and skewers through the biscuits."

And then, in January of 1991, the bottom fell out of everything when Lois Wilkes, Sema's husband of nearly seventy years, passed away. Mrs. Wilkes is still not inclined to talk about her husband's death. Nearly a decade hence, the sense of loss is still raw, unhealed. And yet, she soldiers on, absent her lifemate but all the richer for the seven decades they knew together. These days, Mrs. Wilkes' aches and pains are more numerous, but her workday is much the same as it was fifty years ago.

Each weekday morning when the door swings wide for the first breakfast seating at 8:00, you can bet she'll be there, attired in a blue-and-white seersucker suit come summer, a plaid skirt and jacket come fall. Her presence is

not merely window dressing. Like any good restaurant owner, she has eyes in the back of her head. If a coffee pot runs dry, she's there to refill it. Need more biscuits to sop up that puddle of gravy? Mrs. Wilkes is on the case. And when it comes time to pay the paltry bill, she takes your money, makes your change, and tries her best to sell you a cookbook or three—all as if to say, I'm no relic, and this dining room is no quaint vestige of the past. Make no mistake about it, Mrs. Wilkes and her dining room remain as vital as ever.

A brief lull follows the close of breakfast service at 9:00 or so. Only then does Mrs. Wilkes take a seat and spoon up some creamy grits from one of the white and blue bowls of crockery that dot the table, taking a strip or two of bacon as she goes, and a bit of scrambled eggs for good measure.

By 10:15 or so, the line has begun to form out front. Lunch, known as dinner to all but the most recent generations of Southerners, doesn't begin until 11:00, and yet a gaggle of hopeful eaters is already queued up, snaking back from beneath the furled copper cupola that shades the side door. They are not alone. Dashing in and out of the monkey grass, up and over the roots of the azaleas, a squall of tabby kittens rambles along the herringbone brick sidewalk, skittering this way and that to avoid the heavy tramp of foot traffic.

The air is thick with anticipation, heady with the sweet, chalky scent of fresh-baked biscuits. As the hour draws near, voices pitch an octave or two higher. Men check their wristwatches and pat their bellies. At 11:00 sharp, Linda Wright unlatches the door and bids the first makeshift group of eight welcome, steering them toward the back table where Al Pace, a veteran of nearly forty years at Mrs. Wilkes' table, and Bill Martin, Mrs. Wilkes' son-in-law, await their dining companions.

The oilcloth-draped tables are set with a veritable cornucopia of country cooking: bowls of creamed potatoes spiked with mustard, and collard greens perfumed with fatback; squash casserole bound with crushed cornflakes, and creamed corn scraped straight from the cob; tiny nubs of okra swimming in stewed tomatoes, and pale green butter beans seasoned with ham scraps; and, yes, platter after platter of pepper-flecked fried chicken, vinegar-napped pork ribs, and gooey chicken and dumplings.

An impatient few reach for their rolls of silverware, intent upon eating everything in their sight, but a friendly glance from a neighbor, a raised eyebrow from their mother, and they pull back. When Mrs. Wilkes gives a good shake to her dinner bell and steps to the center of the room, all heads bow, all kitchen clatter ceases. "Good Lord, bless this food to us," she prays. "And us to thy service. Amen."

The next ten minutes are given over to requests for the passing of this bowl or that platter, until, when it seems like the whole table just might break down and cry if they don't get to sink their collective teeth into a drumstick, conversation comes to a halt and the business of eating begins in earnest.

Thirty minutes, two platters of fried chicken, three batches of biscuits, and a round of banana puddings later, the first few diners begin to push back from the table, bidding goodbye to their newfound friends and collecting their plate and glass and silverware to be taken to the kitchen, where Florrie stands at the ready, a scrub brush in one hand, a sweet smile sneaking across her kind face. Seated on a bench by the window, another group of ten watches, eyeing their progress, waiting to take a place at Mrs. Wilkes' table. —*J. T. E.*

When Mrs. Wilkes gives a good shake to her dinner bell and steps to the center of the room, all heads bow, all kitchen clatter ceases.

Desserts

FRESH COCONUT CAKE

Once so much a tradition in the South, Fresh Coconut Cake is now a real rarity except in the more traditional homes, and of course, at Mrs. Wilkes'.

3 eggs, separated
1 1/2 cups sugar
3/4 cup butter
1/2 teaspoon vanilla extract
2 1/4 cups sifted cake flour
2 1/4 teaspoons baking powder
1/2 teaspoon salt
Milk
1 large coconut, grated, reserving milk
Fresh Coconut Cake Frosting (recipe follows)

Preheat the oven to 350°. Beat the egg whites to soft peaks, while gradually adding 1/2 cup of the sugar. In a separate bowl, beat the egg yolks until thick. Cream the butter with the vanilla and beat in the remaining 1 cup sugar. Stir the egg yolks into the butter mixture and cream well. Sift the flour, baking powder, and salt together 3 times. Add enough milk to the reserved coconut milk to make 1 cup liquid. Alternate adding the coconut liquid and flour mixture to the butter mixture. Blend in 1/4 cup of the coconut grating and beat well. Fold in the egg whites. Pour into two 9-inch or three 8-inch layer pans. Bake for 25 to 30 minutes. Frost the cake layers, assemble, and sprinkle with the remaining coconut grating. Yields 1 cake.

FRESH COCONUT CAKE FROSTING

There is no better topping for fresh coconut cake.

2 cups sugar
1 (12-ounce) can evaporated milk
1/2 cup butter
1 teaspoon vanilla extract
1 coconut, grated

Combine the sugar, milk, butter, and vanilla. Cook for about 5 minutes, until the mixture begins to thicken. Mix in the coconut. Frosts one 8- or 9-inch layered cake.

MARCIA'S BOARDINGHOUSE POUND CAKE

MARCIA'S BOARDINGHOUSE POUND CAKE

"The secret is the cream cheese," says Marcia of this super-rich pound cake.

1 (8-ounce) package cream cheese
1 1/2 cups butter, softened
1 tablespoon vanilla extract
6 eggs
3 cups sugar
3 cups cake flour

Cream the cream cheese and butter together. Add the vanilla. While beating, add 2 of the eggs, 1 cup of the sugar, and 1 cup of the flour. Repeat until all of the eggs, sugar, and flour are used. Spray a 16 by 4 by 4 1/2-inch loaf pan with vegetable-oil cooking spray and pour the batter into it. Without preheating the oven, bake at slightly under 300° for about 2 hours. Insert a toothpick into the cake; if it comes out clean, the cake is done. Cool and remove from the pan. Delicious! Serves 20 to 25.
NOTE: When baking pound cakes, never open the oven for a peek—a pound cake is prone to fall when the oven door is opened. Test only after the full cooking time has passed.

Gingerbread

When the temperature starts to drop and thoughts turn to fall, this spicy sweet treat is sure to warm the palate.

1 cup sugar
1/2 cup shortening
2 eggs, beaten
2 teaspoons baking soda
1 cup buttermilk
1 cup molasses
2 teaspoons ground cinnamon
1 1/2 teaspoons ground ginger
1 teaspoon ground cloves
1/4 teaspoon nutmeg
1 teaspoon salt
3 cups all-purpose flour
Whipped cream (optional)
Lemon Sauce (recipe follows) (optional)

Preheat the oven to 365°. Cream the sugar and shortening; add the eggs. Dissolve the baking soda in buttermilk and add to the mixture. Add the molasses, cinnamon, ginger, cloves, nutmeg, salt, and flour. Bake in two 8 by 8 by 2-inch square pans for about 20 minutes. Serve with whipped cream and Lemon Sauce. Yields 32 slices

Lemon Sauce

1 cup sugar
4 tablespoons cornstarch
1/4 teaspoon salt
1 cup water
1 teaspoon grated lemon rind
6 tablespoons lemon juice
2 tablepoons butter or margarine

Combine the sugar, cornstarch, and salt in a small saucepan. Add the water and cook over low heat for 5 minutes, until the mixture thickens and boils. Remove from the heat; add the lemon rind, juice, and butter. Stir until well blended. Cool slightly before serving. Serves 16 to 18.

Red Velvet Cake

A Savannah tradition and Mr. Wilkes' personal favorite for holidays.

2 eggs
1 1/2 cups sugar
1 1/2 cups vegetable oil
1 teaspoon white vinegar
2 1/2 cups cake flour
1 teaspoon baking soda
2 to 3 tablespoons cocoa
1 cup buttermilk
1 teaspoon vanilla extract
5/8 ounce bottle red food coloring
Red Velvet Frosting (recipe follows)

Preheat the oven to 350°. Cream the eggs, sugar, oil, and vinegar. Sift the cake flour, baking soda, and cocoa together. Add the flour mixture to the creamed ingredients while beating. Slowly add the buttermilk. While still beating, add the vanilla and food coloring. Pour into three 8-inch layer pans and bake for about 25 minutes. Press lightly; if the layers are spongy, then the cake is done. Frost the cooled layers, assemble, and frost the top and sides. Serves 12 to 14.

Famous Diners

Over the past fifty-plus years, Mrs. Wilkes has served her share of famous faces. Here she shares a moment with Kevin Spacey who visited Savannah in 1997 during the filming of the movie *Midnight in the Garden of Good and Evil*, in which he starred.

Red Velvet Cake Frosting

1 (8-ounce) package cream cheese, softened
1/2 cup butter or margarine
1 (1-pound) box confectioners' sugar
1 cup chopped pecans
1 teaspoon vanilla extract

Combine the cream cheese and butter and melt over very low heat. Add the sugar, pecans, and vanilla and mix well. If the frosting becomes too thick, add a little milk. Frosts one 8- or 9-inch layered cake.

Chocolate Pound Cake

1/2 cup butter or margarine
1 cup shortening
3 cups sugar
5 eggs
4 heaping teaspoons cocoa
1 teaspoon baking powder
3 cups sifted cake flour
1/2 teaspoon salt
1 cup milk
1 teaspoon vanilla extract

Preheat the oven to 325°. Cream the butter, shortening, and sugar well. Beat in the eggs. Sift the dry ingredients together. Beat the flour mixture, 1 part at a time, into the butter mixture, alternating with the milk, until just blended. Add the vanilla and mix. Pour into a greased 8-inch tube pan lined with waxed paper. Bake for 1 1/2 hours. Frost with your favorite icing. Serves 16 to 20.

Burnt Sugar Frosting

A rarity these days, this frosting is one of Mrs. Wilkes' signatures.

2 1/2 cups sugar
1/3 cup boiling water
1 cup milk
1/2 cup butter or margarine
Pinch of salt
1 teaspoon vanilla extract

Place 1/2 of the cup sugar in a heavy skillet and cook, stirring, over medium heat until melted. Add the boiling water and stir until a syrup forms. Heat the remaining 2 cups sugar and milk. Add the cooked sugar syrup. Cook to the soft ball stage (234° on a candy thermomenter). Cook for 10 minutes without stirring. Add the butter, salt, and vanilla. Beat until thick enough to spread easily. If the frosting becomes stiff, add some milk. Frosts one 8- or 9-inch layered cake.

Georgia Pecan Mist Cake

Yes, you read the ingredients correctly; there is no flour in this cake.

12 egg whites
1/2 teaspoon salt
3 1/2 cups confectioners' sugar
12 egg yolks
3 cups pecans, finely chopped

Preheat the oven to 350°. Beat the whites and salt until foamy. Gradually add the sugar and continue to beat until stiff but not dry. Beat the yolks until thick and fold into the whites. Gently fold in the pecans. Bake in a tube pan for 50 minutes. Freezes well. Serves 16 to 20.

Pecan Whiskey Cake

A Christmas indulgence beyond compare.

1 cup butter or margarine
2 cups sugar
6 eggs, well beaten
4 cups sifted cake flour
4 teaspoons baking powder
2/3 teaspoon salt
2 teaspoons nutmeg
1 cup good aged whiskey
3 cups seedless raisins
4 cups broken pecans

Preheat the oven to 350°. Cream the butter, gradually add the sugar, and cream until fluffy. Add eggs. Beat the mixture well. Sift 3 1/2 cups of the flour, baking powder, salt, and nutmeg together. Alternate adding the flour mixture and whiskey to the creamed mixture. Dredge the raisins and nuts in the remaining 1/2 cup flour. Add to the batter, mixing well. Line two 10 by 4-inch loaf pans with buttered waxed paper or 1 large Bundt pan. Bake for about 1 hour. Test with a toothpick before removing from oven. Serves 24.

Thursday's Blackboard Menu

Fried Chicken

BBQ Chicken

Chicken and Dumplings

Beef Stew

Sausage

Baked Ham

Collard Greens

Snap Beans

Black-Eyed Peas

Squash

Rice and Gravy

Mashed Potatoes

Candied Yams

Pickled Beets

Apple Salad

Macaroni Salad

Pineapple Upside-Down Cake

There is one of these brown-crusted beauties at every Wilkes family reunion.

1 cup butter or margarine
1 cup light brown sugar
1 (15-ounce) can sliced pineapple, drained
Maraschino cherries, halved
1 1/2 cups all-purpose flour
1 cup sugar
2 teaspoons baking powder
1/2 teaspoon salt
2/3 cup milk
1 teaspoon vanilla extract
1 egg

Preheat the oven to 350°. Melt 1/2 cup of the butter in an oblong pan. Top with the brown sugar, pineapple, and cherries. Combine the flour, sugar, baking powder, and salt. Add the remaining 1/2 cup butter, milk, and vanilla. Beat for 2 minutes at medium speed. Add the egg and beat for 2 more minutes. Pour the batter over the pineapple and cherries and bake for 30 to 35 minutes. Serves 10 to 12.

Boardinghouse Trifle

"Our version of the Southern favorite, trifle, is as equally in demand as our banana pudding," declares Margie.

1 (6-ounce) box instant vanilla pudding
1 pound cake or sponge cake
1 teaspoon sherry extract or sherry to taste
2/3 cup whipped cream
1 small jar candied or maraschino cherries, cut up

Make the pudding as directed on the box. Let stand while breaking cake into crumbs. Add the sherry to the pudding and pour over the crumbs. Stir the whipped cream through the mixture and garnish with the cherries. Serves 8.

Sema Says

"I never stop tasting. To be a good cook, you've got to know what good food tastes like."

Strawberry Shortcake

"This is our second most popular dessert, following hard on the heels of Banana Pudding and Boardinghouse Trifle," claims Marcia.

I cup sifted all-purpose flour
I teaspoon baking powder
I/4 teaspoon salt
2 eggs
I cup sugar
2 tablespoons butter or margarine
I/2 cup hot milk
I teaspoon vanilla extract
3 to 4 cups sugared sliced strawberries
Ice cream or whipped cream

Preheat the oven to 350°. Sift the flour, baking powder, and salt together. Beat the eggs until thick and lemon colored. Gradually add the sugar, beating constantly. Quickly fold the flour mixture into the egg mixture. Add the butter to the hot milk. Add the vanilla and stir into the batter. Blend well. Line an 8 by 8 by 2-inch baking pan with waxed paper and pour the batter into it. Bake for 25 to 30 minutes. Remove from the pan to a cooling rack. To serve, cut into squares, and top with the strawberries and ice cream. Serves 6 to 8.

Banana Cream Cake

3 I/2 cups sifted all-purpose flour
3 I/2 teaspoons baking powder
I/2 cup butter or margarine
I I/4 cups sifted granulated sugar
Yolks of 3 eggs, beaten
Whites of 2 eggs, beaten with 4 teaspoons water
3/4 cup milk
Cream Cake Filling (recipe follows)
2 bananas, sliced

Preheat the oven to 350°. Combine the sifted flour and baking powder and sift 3 times. Cream the butter and sugar thoroughly. Add the egg yolks and whites, then alternate adding the flour and milk. Bake in two 8- or 9-inch layer cake pans for about 30 to 35 minutes. Spread the filling on the layers, assemble, and spread the filling on top and garnish with banana slices. Serves 12 to 16.

CREAM CAKE FILLING

2 cups confectioners' sugar
1 tart apple, grated and peeled
White of 1 egg, well beaten

Add the sugar and apple to the egg white and mix. Yields enough for one 8- or 9-inch layered cake.

CARROT CAKE

2 cups all-purpose flour
2 teaspoons baking soda
1 teaspoon salt
3 teaspoons ground cinnamon
4 eggs
2 cups granulated sugar
1 1/2 cups salad oil
3 cups grated carrots
Cream Cheese Frosting (recipe follows)

Preheat the oven to 350°. Sift the flour, baking soda, salt, and cinnamon together. Beat the eggs and mix with the sugar. Add the salad oil. Spoon into the flour mixture. Fold in the carrots. Pour into three 8- or 9-inch layer pans and bake for 35 to 40 minutes. Spread the frosting on the layers, assemble, and spread the frosting on top. Serves 15 to 20.

CREAM CHEESE FROSTING

1 (1-pound) box confectioners' sugar
1/4 cup butter or margarine
1 (8-ounce) package cream cheese, softened
1 cup chopped nuts
1 teaspoon vanilla extract

Cream the sugar, butter, and cream cheese. Fold in the nuts and vanilla. Frosts one 8- or 9-inch layered cake.

MRS. WILKES AND OTHER RECIPIENTS OF THE JAMES BEARD REGIONAL CLASSICS RESTAURANT AWARD.

FRUIT COBBLER

Not many cobblers are as popular for their crust as for the fruit filling. This one is a sure pleaser!

2 cups apples, cherries, or berries, or 2 (16-ounce) cans
   fruit in juice, drained
3 tablespoons butter or margarine
1 tablespoon grated lemon rind
3 tablespoons cornstarch
1 1/2 cups sugar
1 cup sifted flour
1 teaspoon baking powder
1/2 teaspoon salt
1 cup milk
1/4 cup shortening
1 teaspoon vanilla extract
1 egg

Preheat the oven to 350°. Combine the fruit, butter, and lemon rind in a saucepan. Add the cornstarch and 3/4 cup of the sugar. Cook, stirring constantly, until thickened. Pour into a 10 by 6-inch baking dish and let stand while making the topping. Sift the flour, the remaining 3/4 cup sugar, baking powder, and salt into a mixing bowl. Add the milk, shortening, vanilla, and egg. Beat at medium speed for 2 or 3 minutes. Spoon over the fruit mixture in a baking dish. Bake for 40 minutes. Serves 8.

FRUITCAKE

The glaze keeps this old family recipe moist.

4 cups sifted all-purpose flour
1 pound candied cherries
1 pound candied pineapple
1/2 pound chopped sugared dates
2 cups pecans, chopped
1 cup butter or margarine
2 cups sugar
4 eggs
1 1/3 cups buttermilk
1/2 teaspoon baking soda
Fruitcake Glaze (recipe follows)

Preheat the oven to 275°. Sift the flour over the cherries, pineapple, dates, and pecans. Work the flour through using your hands. Cream the butter and sugar. Add the eggs, one at a time, while beating. Add 1 cup of the buttermilk. Mix the remaining 1/3 cup buttermilk with the baking soda and add to the liquid mixture. Pour the liquid mixture over the fruit and mix. The batter will be very thick. Pour in a large tube pan that has been sprayed with vegetable-oil cooking spray. Bake for 2 1/2 hours, or until a toothpick inserted in the center comes out clean. The baking time varies with different ovens. Pour the glaze over the cake while still hot. Leave the cake in the pan until cool. Store covered. Serves 20 to 24.

NOTE: The longer you keep cake, the better it will taste. Good after freezing for later use.

FRUITCAKE GLAZE

2 cups light brown sugar
1 (16-ounce) can frozen orange or lemon juice concentrate

Combine the sugar and juice concentrate and mix until a pouring consistency.

Bread or Biscuit Pudding

One of the frequently asked questions in the '50s was "When will you be serving bread pudding again?"

4 cups biscuit or 2-day-old bread crumbs
1 1/2 cups sugar
1/2 teaspoon nutmeg
3/4 teaspoon ground cinnamon
1 cup shredded coconut
2 1/2 cups crushed fresh pineapple
1 cup raisins
1/2 cup evaporated milk
2 eggs
2 to 4 tablespoons melted butter or margarine

Preheat the oven to 375°. Combine all ingredients and pour into a well-greased baking pan. Bake for 1 hour, or until a toothpick inserted in the pudding comes out clean. Serves 10 to 12.

Banana Pudding

You will find this every day at dessert time at Mrs. Wilkes'. "For a delicious change, we sometimes substitute our pound cake for the vanilla wafers," informs Marcia. This is a special favorite of the Girl Scouts who troop over from the Juliette Gordon Low House, birthplace of the founder of the Girl Scouts of America.

1 (6-ounce) box instant vanilla pudding
1 (7 1/4-ounce) box vanilla wafers
4 bananas, sliced
Meringue (recipe follows)

Preheat the oven to 375°. Make the pudding according to the directions on the box. Arrange the wafers, sliced bananas, and pudding in layers in a 2-quart casserole, ending with a layer of pudding on top. This will make 3 layers. Spread the meringue gently over the top. Bake for 15 minutes. Serves 8.
NOTE: For a quicker version of this recipe, use pudding as directed on box and place a layer of whipped cream on top.

FAMOUS DINERS

During the 1996 Summer Olympic sailing competitions in Savannah, a special dinner at Mrs. Wilkes' was hosted by the Olympic Committee in recognition of Walter Cronkite.

MERINGUE

2 egg whites
1/8 teaspoon salt
4 tablespoons sugar
1/4 teaspoon vanilla extract

Beat the egg whites and salt until frothy. Add 1 tablespoon of sugar at a time and vanilla, and beat until the meringue is stiff.

AMBROSIA

1 quart orange sections, sliced out from pulp
1 cup thinly sliced bananas
1/2 cup pineapple tidbits
1/2 cup maraschino cherries
1/2 cup chopped pecans
1/2 cup shredded coconut
1 cup sugar (more if oranges are bitter)

Mix all of the ingredients thoroughly. Chill. Delicious served topped with sweetened whipped cream. Serves 12.

Fried Chicken

Baked Chicken and Dressing

Beef Stew

BBQ Ribs

Baked Ham

Collard Greens

Snap Beans

English Peas and Noodles

Baked Beans

Potato Salad

Candied Yams

Pickled Beets

Coleslaw

Macaroni and Cheese

Squash

LEMON SQUARES

A tart Southern treat.

1 cup butter or margarine, softened
1/4 cup confectioners' sugar, plus extra for dusting
2 cups plus 2 tablespoons all-purpose flour
3 eggs, beaten
1/4 teaspoon salt
1 cup granulated sugar
4 tablespoons lemon juice
1 tablespoon grated lemon rind
1/2 teaspoon baking powder

Preheat the oven to 350°. To make the crust, cream the butter and confectioners' sugar; add 2 cups of the flour to make a dough. Pat out in a 9 by 9-inch pan. Bake for 15 minutes. Mix the eggs, salt, granulated sugar, lemon juice and rind, remaining 2 tablespoons flour, and baking powder. Pour over the crust and bake for 20 to 25 minutes. When cool, dust with confectioners' sugar. Cut into small squares. Yields about 36 to 42 squares.

PRALINE COOKIES

1/2 cup soft butter or margarine
1 1/2 cups dark brown sugar
1 egg, beaten
1 1/2 cups sifted all-purpose flour
1 teaspoon vanilla extract
1 cup coarsely chopped pecans

Cream the butter, sugar, and egg. Add the flour, vanilla, and pecans and mix. Refrigerate until the dough is easy to handle. Preheat the oven to 375°. Shape the dough into 1-inch balls and place them 3 inches apart on a greased cookie sheet. Using the bottom of a tumbler covered with damp cheesecloth, flatten the balls till 1/8-inch thick. Bake for 12 minutes or until done. Yields 3 dozen.

Standard Piecrust

Every good pie filling deserves a flaky foundation, and this is the best there is.

1 1/4 cups all-purpose flour
1/2 teaspoon salt
1/2 cup shortening
2 to 3 tablespoons cold water

Sift the flour and salt into a medium mixing bowl. Cut in the shortening until well blended. Sprinkle in the water 1 tablespoon at a time, until well blended and the dough cleans the sides of the bowl. Yields one 8- or 9-inch piecrust.
NOTE: For a double-crusted pie, substitute 2 cups all-purpose flour, 1 teaspoon salt, 3/4 cup shortening, and 5 to 6 tablespoons water.

No Roll Piecrust

When your recipe calls for a baked crust, you can't find a quicker, easier piecrust than this one.

1 1/2 cups self-rising flour
1 teaspoon salt
1 1/2 teaspoons sugar
2 tablespoons milk
1/2 cup cooking oil

Preheat the oven to 375°. Combine the flour, salt, and sugar in a pie pan. Mix the milk with the cooking oil and pour over the flour. Mix with a fork. Using your hands, pat out as thin as desired for the crust. If the recipe calls for an already baked crust, bake until brown. Yields one 8- or 9-inch piecrust.

Graham Cracker Piecrust

1 1/4 cups graham cracker crumbs (about 15 crackers)
2 tablespoons sugar
1/4 cup butter or margarine, melted

Preheat the oven to 350°. Combine the cracker crumbs and sugar in bowl. Add the butter and mix until well blended. If desired, save 1/4 cup mixture for topping. Press the mixture firmly against the bottom and sides of the pie pan. Bake for 10 minutes. Yields one 8- or 9-inch piecrust.
NOTE: Ginger, chocolate, or vanilla wafers may be substituted for the graham crackers, but you can omit the sugar.

Fresh Peach Pie

5 or 6 fresh peaches, peeled and sliced
4 slices white bread
1 egg, beaten
1 1/4 cups sugar
2 tablespoons flour
1/2 cup butter or margarine, melted
Vanilla ice cream

Preheat the oven to 350°. Cover the bottom of an 8 by 8-inch baking dish with the peach slices. Trim the edges from the bread. Cut the bread into strips and place over the peaches. Combine the egg, sugar, flour, and butter. Pour the mixture over the peaches and bread. Bake for 25 to 30 minutes. Top with vanilla ice cream. Serves 8 to 10.

Egg Custard Pie

This is a rich and soothing Wilkes family favorite.

4 eggs, well beaten
1 3/4 cups sugar
1/4 cup butter or margarine, melted
1/2 cup self-rising flour
2 cups milk
1 tablespoon vanilla extract

Preheat the oven to 375°. Combine the egg, sugar, butter, flour, milk, and vanilla. Pour into a greased 9- or 10-inch deep dish pie pan. Bake for 30 minutes, or until brown. Let set until cool. Serves 8 to 10.
NOTE: For coconut pie, add 2 (7-ounce) cans coconut. For fruit pie, add 1 small can crushed pineapple or 1 cup mashed peaches.

BLACKBERRY PIE

This Southern favorite is so good served warm with whipped cream or vanilla ice cream.

3 cups blackberries, mashed, reserving juice
1 cup sugar
3 tablespoons all-purpose flour
1/2 cup butter or margarine, melted
Double Standard Piecrust (page 163, see Note)

Preheat the oven to 425°. If desired, strain the blackberries to remove the seeds. Mix the sugar and flour together. Add the butter and blackberries with juice. Pour into 1 of the piecrusts. Slit the remaining crust to allow the steam to escape and cover the pie. Bake for 40 to 45 minutes. Serves 8 to 10.

PECAN PIE

3 eggs
1 cup light corn syrup
1/2 cup sugar
1 teaspoon vanilla extract
Pinch of salt
3 tablespoons butter or margarine
1 cup broken pecans
Standard Piecrust (page 163) or other
    unbaked crust

Preheat the oven to 350°. Combine the eggs and corn syrup and mix thoroughly. Add the sugar, vanilla, salt, butter, and pecans. Stir well. Pour into the unbaked crust. Bake for 45 to 60 minutes. Serves 8 to 10.

"I took a taxi to Mrs. Wilkes'. When I told the driver where I was going he handed me his card. 'What's that for?' I asked. 'If you're going to Mrs. Wilkes', you're not going to feel like walking back. Give me a call when you get through eating.'"

—LEWIS GRIZZARD,
Atlanta Journal-Constititutuion,
February 24, 1986

Sweet Potato Pie

No Georgia cookbook can call itself such without a special sweet potato pie recipe.

1 cup brown sugar
1 teaspoon ground cinnamon
1/4 teaspoon ground cloves
1/4 teaspoon ground nutmeg
1/4 teaspoon salt
2 eggs
1 2/3 cups evaporated milk
1 1/2 cups boiled, peeled sweet potatoes beaten with mixer
Standard Piecrust (page 163) or other unbaked crust
Whipped Cream

Preheat the oven to 425°. Combine the sugar, cinnamon, cloves, nutmeg, and salt. Beat the eggs with the milk and combine with the sugar mixture and sweet potatoes until smooth. Heat in a saucepan until almost boiling and pour into the unbaked crust. Bake for 15 minutes, reduce the heat to 350° and continue to bake for 15 to 20 minutes, until or until a knife inserted comes out clean. Serve with whipped cream. Serves 8 to 10.

Fresh Strawberry Pie

Mrs. Wilkes' strawberries come from Bamboo Farm and Coastal Garden. At the peak of the strawberry season (usually middle to late spring), Mrs. Wilkes' donates pound cakes to their annual fundraiser, Sunday Supper in the Strawberry Patch.

1 quart strawberries, washed and hulled
1 cup plus 2 to 3 tablespoons sugar
2 1/2 or 3 tablespoons cornstarch
2 tablespoons lemon juice
Red food coloring
No Roll Piecrust (page 163) or other baked piecrust
1/2 pint whipping cream

Put half of the strawberries in a saucepan and crush. Mix 1 cup of the sugar and cornstarch, and add to the crushed strawberries along with the lemon juice. Cook over medium heat until the mixture thickens. Cool. Add a few drops of red food coloring. Cut the remaining strawberries into halves and mix with the cooked mixture. Pour into the baked crust and chill. Whip the cream and the remaining 2 to 3 tablespoons sugar in a small bowl until thick. Place a dollop of cream on each pie slice before serving. Serves 8 to 10.

PEANUT BUTTER PIE

Family friend Gerry Griffin says that she keeps one of these in the freezer all the time, ready for unexpected company.

1 (3-ounce) package cream cheese, softened
1 cup confectioners' sugar
1/2 cup creamy peanut butter
1/4 cup evaporated milk
Graham Cracker Piecrust (page 164)
1/3 cup peanuts, chopped
1 1/2 cups whipped cream

Whip the cream cheese until fluffy. Beat in the sugar and peanut butter. Slowly add the milk, blending well into the mixture. Pour into the piecrust. Sprinkle with chopped peanuts. Chill until firm. Serve with whipped cream. Serves 8 to 10.

CHOCOLATE PECAN PIE

So rich, you'll think you can afford a second piece!

2/3 cup evaporated milk
2 tablespoons butter or margarine
1 (12-ounce) package semisweet chocolate chips
2 eggs
1 cup light corn syrup
2 tablespoons flour
1/4 teaspoon salt
1 cup whole pecans
1 teaspoon vanilla extract
Standard Piecrust (page 163) or other unbaked crust

Preheat the oven to 375˚. Place the milk, butter, and chocolate in a saucepan. Cook, stirring, over low heat until melted. Combine the eggs, corn syrup, flour, and salt. Add to to the chocolate mixture. Stir in the pecans and vanilla. Pour into the unbaked crust. Bake for about 45 minutes. Serves 8 to 10.

FAMOUS DINERS

Charlize Theron, in Savannah in 2000 to film Robert Redford's *Legend of Bagger Vance*, with Mrs. Wilkes' great-grandson, Ryon Thompson, who works at the restaurant with his family. "I was like, bring it on!" Theron later told an interviewer in New York. "More fried chicken and peach cobbler, please!"

LEMON MERINGUE PIE

This is Marcia Thompson's favorite pie—she loves that mile-high meringue!

1 3/4 cups sugar
1/4 cup cornstarch
1/8 teaspoon salt
1 1/4 cups warm water
Grated rind of 1 lemon
1/4 cup lemon juice
3 egg yolks, slightly beaten
1 tablespoon butter or margarine
No Roll Piecrust (page 163) or other baked crust
Meringue (recipe follows)

In the top of a double boiler, combine the sugar, cornstarch, and salt. Slowly stir in the water, then the lemon rind and juice, egg yolks, and butter. Cook, stirring, until smooth and thick enough to mound when dropped from spoon. Remove from the heat. Cool thoroughly. Preheat the oven to 350˚. Spoon the filling into the cooled piecrust. Bake for 12 to 15 minutes. Remove from the oven and decrease the heat to 300˚. Let the pie cool. Spread the meringue on top and bake for 15 to 20 minutes, or until golden on top. Serves 8.

MERINGUE

1/4 teaspoon salt
3 egg whites
6 tablespoons sugar
1/2 teaspoon almond extract
1/2 teaspoon vanilla extract

Add the salt to the egg whites and beat until stiff. Gradually fold in the sugar and add the almond and vanilla extracts. Yields enough for 1 pie.
NOTE: For meringue shells, preheat the oven to 225˚, then make the meringue. Drop the meringue on a greased baking sheet. Mash out with the back of a spoon and make a hollow in the middle to hold the filling. Bake for 1/2 hour. Cool before adding your favorite filling. Yields 8 to 10 shells.

DIVINITY

At Christmastime, add slices of red and green candied cherries for a special touch.

3 cups sugar
3/4 cup white corn syrup
1/4 cup water
3 egg whites
Pinch of salt
1 cup chopped pecans

Cook the sugar, corn syrup, and water until mixture reaches the hard ball stage. This is an almost brittle ball when dropped in cold water; if using candy thermometer, cook to 265°. Cook, uncovered, gently without stirring. Beat the egg whites until stiff and add the salt. Slowly pour the syrup into the egg whites, while beating. If desired, add your choice of food coloring while beating in the syrup. Beat until thick and creamy. Add the nuts and drop by teaspoonfuls onto waxed paper. Cool. Yields about 4 dozen.

SWEET POTATO AND SQUASH PIE

1 small butternut squash, peeled, seeded, and cut up
3 or 4 medium sweet potatoes, peeled and cut up
1 cup sugar
3 eggs
3/8 cup butter or margarine, melted
1 teaspoon vanilla extract
1/2 teaspoon salt
1 1/4 teaspoons cinnamon
1 teaspoon nutmeg
Standard Piecrust (page 163) or other unbaked crust

Preheat the oven to 350°. In a saucepan, add the squash and sweet potatoes to a small amount of boiling water and cook until tender. Drain and return to the pot. Mash, add the remaining ingredients, and mix until well blended. If the mixture seems too thick, add some milk. Pour into the piecrust and bake for 30 minutes. Serves 8.

Carolyn's Sugared Peanuts

2 cups shelled dry peanuts (not green)
1 cup sugar
1/2 cup water

Preheat the oven to 300°. Boil the peanuts and sugar in the water until the water cooks out and the peanuts begin to look sugary. Be careful not to burn the nuts. Spread them out on a flat pan and bake for 15 minutes. Stir and bake for an additional 15 minutes. Yields 2 cups.

Spiced Pecans

"I used to make my treehouse among the pecan trees on our family farm," reminisces Margie.

2 cups sugar
1 teaspoon cinnamon
1 teaspoon vanilla extract
1/2 cup water
1 teaspoon butter or margarine
1 pound shelled pecans

Cook the sugar, cinnamon, vanilla, water, and butter until the mixture spins a thread (about 228° on candy thermometer). Add the nuts and stir quickly. Turn onto waxed paper and separate into large clumps. Cool. Yields 1 pound.

Index